YOUR TOWNS & CITIES IN W

WATFORD

1939-

EUGENIA RUSSELL
AND
QUENTIN RUSSELL

Pen & Sword
MILITARY

First published in Great Britain in 2019 by
Pen & Sword Military
An imprint of
Pen & Sword Books Limited
Yorkshire - Philadelphia

ISBN 978 1 47389 1 708

A CIP catalogue record for this book is available from the British Library

Printed and bound in the UK
by TJ International Ltd, Padstow, Cornwall

Pen & Sword Books Limited incorporates the imprints of Atlas,
Archaeology, Aviation, Discovery, Family History, Fiction, History, Maritime,
Military, Military Classics, Politics, Select, Transport, True Crime, Air World,
Frontline Publishing, Leo Cooper, Remember When, Seaforth Publishing,
The Praetorian Press, Wharncliffe Local History, Wharncliffe Transport,
Wharncliffe True Crime and White Owl.

For a complete list of Pen & Sword titles please contact
PEN & SWORD BOOKS LIMITED
47 Church Street, Barnsley, South Yorkshire S70 2AS, United Kingdom
E-mail: enquiries@pen-and-sword.co.uk
Website: www.pen-and-sword.co.uk

Or
PEN AND SWORD BOOKS
1950 Lawrence Rd, Havertown, PA 19083, USA
E-mail: Uspen-and-sword@casematepublishers.com
Website: www.penandswordbooks.com

Contents

CHAPTER ONE

Watford between the Wars

No corner of Europe escaped the devastating effects of the Great War. Its impact was profound, changing individual lives and transforming attitudes to society that would shape the future. Once the dust had settled on the peace celebrations of 1918, the feeling of 'never again' was accompanied by a desire to create a brave new progressive world. The image of the survivors throwing off the past by partying their way through the roaring '20s was mainly an American phenomenon, for their immediate post-war prosperity was not shared in Britain where the interwar period was generally one of economic depression. Nevertheless this did not stint the general desire for regeneration and local authorities attempted to fulfil Prime Minister Lloyd George's promise to the returning soldiers that they would come back to 'a country fit for heroes to live in'. In consequence, the tentative social welfare changes that had been interrupted by the war were resumed with renewed vigour and new initiatives embarked on.

No one anticipated that the peace was to be short-lived, just sufficient time for a new generation to grow mature enough to fill the ranks when duty called again twenty-one years later. But the peace was long enough for significant changes to be set in motion before the mood turned sour. At first, the sombre mood of loss and sacrifice was tempered by the conviction that international relations would be conducted differently in future. Remembrance Day parades became an annual feature of British life in every town and village, accompanied by the laying of wreaths at the local war memorials. In 1924, to mark the tenth anniversary of the beginning of the war, an open-air Armistice Day service with a two-minute silence was held outside the Watford Council office. But it was widely thought that this dwelling on the past would not be enough to ensure that the 'war to end all wars' would live up to its description; a political solution was necessary. As a result of the Paris Peace Conference that brought the war to an end, the League of Nations was formed in 1920 with the intention of curbing the arms race and trying to solve international disputes through arbitration and negotiation. In Watford the local branch of the League of Nations Union took its own active role in trying to prevent a second conflict. A fervent supporter and vice-president of the Watford branch was the well-known Irish artist James Doyle Penrose, who lived at Oxhey Grange from 1908 until his death in 1932. Penrose was involved in Liberal politics and an elder in the Watford Quaker meeting, affiliations that underpinned his duties as a member of the Hertfordshire Commission for Peace. He held an annual International Garden Party at the Grange with guests from amongst his Indian friends and including the Chinese ambassador. Despite such efforts, the international situation was worsened with the rise of fascism, and the peace activists' frustrations turned to more disruptive tactics. In 1935, following the Italian invasion of Abyssinia, members of the Watford League now felt justified in using the Remembrance Day parades as a focus for anti-war demonstrations.

Penrose was also treasurer of the Watford Temperance Council of Christian Churches and a supporter of the Adult School in Derby Road. His community interests reflected the social concerns of the time. Aware of the poor living conditions of his workers, he improved the housing on his vast estate and was largely responsible for the modern appearance of the area known as Watford Heath. After his death part of the estate was sold for housing, initiating the suburban development of Carpenders Park that would continue in the 1950s. Drunkenness and housing were seen as major problems in the aftermath of the war. Hard as it might be to imagine today, as most of Watford's old drinking establishments have disappeared, there was a pub virtually every few yards the length of the High Street from the Wheatsheaf at Bushey Arches to The Dog in Hempstead Road (both no longer in existence).

Politically, Watford, a constituency that then included the urban districts of Bushey, Chorleywood, Rickmansworth and part of the Rural District of Watford, favoured the Conservatives. Denis Herbert, who lived locally in a Victorian villa in Clarendon Road (demolished 2015), held the seat from the general election of December 1918 until 1943 when he was raised to the peerage as Baron Hemingford. As a result of the Representation of the People Act brought in by Lloyd George, the 1914 election was the first in which all men over the age of 21 and women over 30 meeting the minimum property qualifications could vote. Lloyd George's record of strong leadership against Germany and his promises of social and economic progress went down well with voters in what was termed a 'khaki election' and his Liberal-Conservative Coalition swept to a landslide victory. While the war veterans held on to their memories through associations such as the Comrades of the Great War Club at the British Legion headquarters in St Albans Road, a new generation hoped for a different future. Although the returning ex-soldiers might replace women war-workers in many jobs, the clock could not be turned back; the previous gendered definition of the roles of men and women had been eroded forever. The following April, the first woman councillor, Mrs Amy Wheelwright, was elected to Bushey Urban District Council. In Watford the completion in 1925 of the Trade Union Hall, built by voluntary labour, reflected the growing industrial base of the area, and on 1 January 1931 it was visited by the Labour prime minister Ramsay MacDonald, who received a rapturous welcome; a sign of things to come.

The character of South West Hertfordshire was changing. The decline in importance of rural life in the area meant the old market town of Watford was being replaced by a growing modern one dependent on industry and drawn ever closer into the orbit of London. In 1922, Watford was upgraded from an Urban District to a Municipal Borough, with its own mayor, borough council and greater authority. The bid for its Charter had been supported by George Villiers, 6th Earl of Clarendon, and he became the town's first mayor. The war had highlighted the shortcomings of local public services and the new council embarked on an ambitious programme of civic rejuvenation during a period of austerity, high unemployment and low wages. In 1924, a Town Improvement Committee was convened to oversee the expansion of the utility services, electricity, water and sewage. Gas was still in private hands – the Watford and St Albans gas companies amalgamated in 1930 taking in the Elstree and Borehamwood company and expanding to include Rickmansworth in 1934. Watford was the first local authority to electrify all their streetlights. In September 1929, the incoming mayor, Alderman F.J.B. Hemmings, outlined the Council's ambition to the *Daily Mail* saying that Watford would become a model town planned on scientific lines.

In 1919, the old Urban District Council had acquired 'The Elms', an eighteenth-century mansion in ten acres of land on the corner of Hempstead Road and Rickmansworth Road at the junction with St. Albans Road and the High Street, known as The Four Cross Roads. The site was earmarked for a new hospital, baths and town hall. The paddock facing Rickmansworth Road provided the site for the Peace Memorial Hospital which superseded the no longer adequate (District) Cottage Hospital in Vicarage Road. The deficiencies of the old hospital had become apparent under the pressure of treating the war-wounded. £90,000 was raised by public appeal and the new hospital was opened by the Princess Royal, Princess Mary, in 1925. A further increase in health-care capacity was made in 1930 when the Council converted the old Watford Union Workhouse at 30 Vicarage Road into a hospital – Shrodells (meaning 'shrubberies') Public Assistance Institution. In addition, in 1935, the small temporary Maternity Ward in the Nurses Training Home at Southfield House, jointly managed by Hertfordshire County Council and Hertfordshire County Nursing Association, was given a permanent residence as the Watford Maternity Home at 21 King Street. By the late 1930s the rapid expansion of the town meant the Peace Memorial Hospital needed a further £70,000 to be raised from the public for an extension. Completing the picture of the Council's plans for the area of Hempstead Road, in 1928 a new purpose-designed Central Public Library was built next to the Maternity and Child Welfare Clinic in Little Nascot house (1874, rebuilt 1941), and the quaint outdoor swimming experience of the lido where the Five Arches railway viaduct crossed the River Colne was improved with the opening of the Central Swimming Baths (1933). In keeping with these improvements the previous centre of local government at Upton House in the High Street was moved to its new site at The Elms. The Elms House was demolished and the foundation stone of a new Town Hall was laid in May 1938. Designed by Charles Cowles Voysey at a cost of £186,000 it was officially opened on 5 January 1940 by Lord Clarendon.

The Central Public Library, which cost £20,000, part funded by the Carnegie United Kingdom Trust, was relocated from the site it had occupied in Queen's Road since 1877. Watford was already a pioneer in technical education, but in 1922 the Council began a restructuring of the School of Art, Science and Commerce. A Junior Technical School was established in the old public library building in 1929, and the following year the two schools were brought together to form the Watford Technical School. This proved a successful move with high employment rates being achieved among leavers in the skilled trades. In the 1930s the school became a prestigious selective school competing with but not surpassing Watford Boys Grammar School. With this expansion, the Queen's Road site was thought no longer good enough and plans were laid for a new college to be built in Hempstead Road. The growth of the town meant a greater requirement for schooling and new schools were built that reflected the latest in educational theory. Leggatts Way School, a secondary school for boys and girls aged 11 to 14 built in 1922, complied with the new ideas on education, child development and the need for specialist teaching as outlined in the Hadow Reports (1923-33) which proposed dividing education instruction into primary and secondary as opposed to provision under the all-inclusive roof of the elementary school.

The increase in population had other effects on town life. A new Post Office had to be built in 1932 in Market Street to replace the 'temporary' one in Queen's Road established in 1880 that was no longer adequate, and the advent of the era of the motorcar meant something urgently needed to be done about the roads. The need to do work on the High Street was exacerbated by the serious requirements to improve the sewage system and after the laying of new pipes it was tarmaced in 1923. Using their powers of compulsory purchase, the Council then generally improved and widened the central roads. The northern end of the High Street known as The Parade, and the area around the Pond, was redeveloped during the late '20s and early '30s. Parts of The Parade were built on the site of a market garden and nursery and the area was turned from what had been a relatively open space occupied by large houses with gardens into a more urban environment with the addition of commercial buildings. The Mansion House (a Grade II listed building, now Monmouth House and The Platts) built in 1612 by Sir Robert Carey, Earl of Monmouth, as a dower house, was modernised into retail outlets and business premises and next door the Tudor style Monmouth Place was constructed with materials from the demolished Cassiobury House (more of which later). An early occupant of the redevelopment was the Gas Showroom at no. 149, opened in 1930, and to promote the significant expansion in the use of domestic electricity at a time when around only a quarter of houses were supplied, an Electricity Showroom followed in a large 'set piece' structure in 1938 at no. 135 by the Pond. The gas showroom subsequently moved to Clarendon Road, another area that was fast losing its residential quality. The ubiquity of the motorcar required a car park, and this was provided in 1932 on the site of a large house known as The Shrubbery and in 1936 the 'The Four Cross Roads' became a roundabout.

Nothing had defined the character of the town more than the traditional Tuesday and Saturday market, but the width of the High Street was no longer sufficient to accommodate it and the increase in traffic. In 1926 the Council acquired the rights, once held by the Earl of Essex and St Albans Abbey, from Hugh Flint, an auctioneer, and the stallholders were transferred to a new site in Red Lion Yard in 1928. This became a covered market. The cattle market off Marlborough Road was moved to Stones Alley off Market Street until its closure in 1959. The nature of the central core was rapidly changing with an influx of new shops and national retail chains. The Essex Arms Hotel in Market Place next to Lloyds Bank was demolished in 1931 and replaced by Timothy Whites the chemist and an extension to Cawdell's drapery store. Trewins, established in Queen's Road since the 1880s, was bought out by Selfridges, and Marks & Spencers took over the Penny Bazaar in the High Street (1928). In the early 1920s, Boots, W.H. Smiths, Sainsbury's, the Co-op and the International Stores all moved into premises.

To the three pre-war cinemas – the Central Hall (King Street), the Empire (Merton Road) and the Electric Coliseum (St Albans Road) – was added The Super in 1921, which replaced the roller-skating rink in Clarendon Road. Others followed, specifically designed to show the new 'talkies'. The custom-built Plaza (taken over by the Odeon in 1936, now demolished) opened near the Pond on 8 July 1929 with *The Singing Fool* staring Al Jolson. Will Hay in person opened The Gaumont at 65 The Parade in 1937; it boasted a Wurlitzer organ. A further Odeon on St Albans Road opened the same year. The *Watford Observer* reported that after rejecting the concept five times, Watford Council eventually agreed in 1938 to poll the population on whether cinemas should open on Sundays. The public voted 9,600 to 6,900 in favour. Because of the competition the Palace Theatre changed from being a Palace of Varieties to a repertory theatre under the management of Andrew Melville.

Away from the centre many roads were still muddy tracks even in the late 1930s and their upgrading was a more lengthy process. Generally traffic congestion was becoming a problem in the London area, so to ease the situation central government proposed a 'radial' road scheme around the capital. The scheme was never fully realised, but parts of the northern section, known as the North Orbital Road, were upgraded around Leavesden, St Albans and Park Street. In 1932, a section between St Albans Road, by the

Three Horse Shoes, and the Watford Bypass was opened (A405). The Watford Bypass or North-Western Avenue (A500, from 1950 redesignated the A41) began development in 1924 to connect Stanmore with the Hempstead Road at Hunton Bridge, the northern end of the old main road (the old A41) to Aylesbury that had passed through the town. The new road bypassing Bushey and Watford to the east was eventually extended south to avoid Edgware and Cricklewood in 1935. Paradoxically road improvements meant to take traffic away from the central area ultimately only increased traffic as new industry was attracted in by the improvements.

The Grand Junction Canal (known as the Grand Union Canal from 1927) that tracked the River Gade through Cassiobury Park was still an important commercial link between London and Birmingham, but it was being superseded by its more modern competitors. Rail links were improving, and the pre-war fear of the people of Watford and Bushey being swallowed up by Greater London became real again. In 1925, the electrified extension of the Metropolitan railway from Moor Park brought Rickmansworth within twenty-four minutes of Baker Street. Part of the Metroland dream of commuter suburban living, improvements that went hand in hand with housing developments along the route, Watford Metropolitan Station followed in November that year, opening in Cassiobury Park Avenue to the west of the Park. The originally intended terminus was to have been 'Watford Central' in the High Street, but the Council had turned down the planned route through the Park to the Hempstead Road and tunnelling to the High Street had proved too expensive. A bus service was then required to link the station to the centre and the line suffered from competition from the existing Bakerloo line from Watford Junction and Watford High Street. On land purchased north of Edgware, London Transport began construction work in the late 1930s on part of its 'New Works Programme' known as the 'Northern Heights' project; the intended electrified extension of the Northern line from Edgware to Bushey Heath. The plan was suspended with the outbreak of war. From 1920, the London General Omnibus Company provided another route from Watford to Harrow and Kilburn and there was competition from other bus companies for routes into the town centre and beyond. A number of these smaller companies were amalgamated in 1933 by the London Passenger Transport Board.

The growth of the town exacerbated the already urgent need for good quality housing. Lack of housing was a general immediate post-war problem, and the government encouraged the building of houses for ex-servicemen and key workers. Local schemes were inaugurated throughout the Watford area and new housing projects began as soon as land became available. A major factor in the town's development was the sale of the Cassiobury Estate. Before the First World War much of the life of rural Hertfordshire had been dominated by the big landowners and to the north of the town there were two large estates, the Cassiobury Estate, the seat of the Earls of Essex, and that of the Earl of Clarendon centred on The Grove. In 1894, a blow was dealt to the established order when death duties were introduced by the Liberal government. The glory days of the large country house were numbered and by the 1920s the gentry were struggling to maintain their residences. Cassiobury had been the Capel family's country retreat since the 1540s, and its remodelled Tudor house famous for its interiors was Watford's most distinguished building. As *Country Life* magazine reported in 1910, it was

> *...set in great and delightful grounds and surrounded by a grandly timbered park. Therein is peace and quiet; the aloofness of the old-country home far from the haunts of men reigns there still, and Watford and its rows of villas and its busy streets is forgotten as soon as the lodge gates are passed.*

Cassiobury Park's demise had been slow. George Devereux de Vere Capell, the 7th Earl of Essex, began selling the land off for a mixture of building developments that included villas, terraced houses, shops and factories in 1897. By 1909, he had already sold 184 acres to the Urban District Council for housing and use as a public park. In 1912 Watford Boys Grammar School moved to a site in the former grounds and just before the outbreak of war in 1914 the Great Central Railway took an additional five and a half acres of the estate for development. The final act came when the Earl died in 1916 after being hit by a taxi and Cassiobury House was left empty. Lady Essex, the former American heiress Adele Grant, and her son were obliged to sell the remainder of the estate and the house in 1922 to pay the death duties. During a spectacular ten-day sale in June the family's impressive collection of art treasures, furniture and lavish interior fixtures and fittings, including four separate libraries, were disposed of; but the house proved more problematic. Adele was unable to find a buyer before further tragedy struck and she died of a heart attack the following month. The house stood empty until it was bought by a group of local businessmen for its development potential. It was then stripped, its Grinling Gibbons carvings joining the rest of the collections that had been split between a number of museums and private collectors around the world, mainly in the United States. The house remained derelict until it was demolished in 1927. Some of its bricks were used to build Monmouth Place in Watford, others travelled as far as America where at least one house was built from them. Cassiobury Park, the area of the former estate owned by the Council, acquired a bandstand that fell into disuse with the outbreak of war (dismantled, relocated and then re-erected), a fountain (now gone), the Pavillion Tea Rooms and a paddling pool (replaced by a new pool in the 1980s). The Council also acquired the area of Whippendell Wood in 1935. Little Cassiobury, an estate dower house on Hempstead Road, was obtained by Hertfordshire County Council by compulsory purchase order in 1937. The house was preserved, but the grounds were to be where the new College of Technology was to be built replacing the Watford Technical School in Queen's Road; progress was stalled by the outbreak of war. Russell's, another early eighteenth-century estate dower house, was occupied by Lewis Evans, the antiquarian brother of Sir Arthur Evans, the famous excavator of Knossos in Crete. In 1920 the house was taken over by the Maharaja Sayajirao Gaekwad III of Baroda who was looking for a permanent residence in England. He used the house to hold garden parties to which he would invite such notables as Lord Birkenhead and various Conservative party supporters. The Maharaja died in 1939.

The sale of Cassiobury House, for so long the symbol of local prestige and power, was a portent of things to come. The power of the landed gentry was waning in the new social order and as other large houses and estates were sold and broken up, the gentry began to lose its grip on local affairs. The Earl of Clarendon moved from The Grove to his London home in the early 1920s, and the house was leased out to various occupants as a gardening school, a health centre, a riding school and a girl's boarding school. It was eventually sold in 1936 to avoid Estate Duty. The Equity & Law Life Assurance Company purchased the estate as a capital asset, holding it until May 1939 when they sold it for £80,000 to Lineside Estates, a subsidiary company of the London, Midland & Scottish Railway Company. As the future of such properties hung in the balance, no one realised the important role they would play in events to come. In the rural environs there was Bucknalls, built in 1855 in what was then rolling countryside near Leavesden. It was acquired as the important Building Research Station, today the Building Research Establishment (BRE). In Bushey, then still semi-rural with a population of around 9,000, the significant number of large estates and houses of the wealthy that had characterised the area no longer remained in private hands. Bushey Hall, once the fifteenth-century home of Thomas Montecute, the Earl of Salisbury, passed through a number of owners until it was demolished and rebuilt on a new site as a mock-Jacobean extravaganza by Edward Marjoribanks in 1865. The costs were such that Marjoribanks was forced to sell in 1877 and it became a hydrotherapeutic establishment, or health farm, and then a high-class country hotel with a golf club in the former grounds. Requisitioned for officer training by the Household Brigade during the war, it reverted to its former use in the interwar period. It was either debt or death that usually forced the issue. When Adelbert Wellington Brownlow-Cust, 3rd Earl of Brownlow, died in 1921, Ashridge Park near Berkhamsted was split up, the grounds being taken over by the National Trust, and a Golf Club and the house becoming a 'college of citizenship' for the Conservative Party. It was here that the Territorials had been training on the eve of the Great War. On the death in 1932 of Vicary Gibbs, politician, financier and third son of the 1st Baron Aldenham, Aldenham House and its grounds were turned into a country club.

These developments did not solve the Council's critical need to deal with Watford's poor housing stock and the pressure to acquire land to accommodate the town's rapid growth. The population had risen from 40,939 in 1911 to 45,910 in 1921; by 1931 it was 56,802. The programme of slum clearance and house building that had begun before 1914 was resumed. In 1920 it was reckoned that Watford required around 2,000 new houses, including 500 to replace houses in unsanitary areas. The medieval living conditions of the overcrowded and squalid cobbled 'courts' around St Mary's Church between the High Street and Market Street or those of the run-down properties in the numerous alleys had not been fully addressed. Ballard's Buildings, which had been built to house the 'navvies' during the period of railway development, had a particularly bad reputation. In 1924, the slum clearance began. New Street, which ran from Market Place to Church Street and contained the notorious Ballard's Buildings, was demolished in 1926. Between 1924 and 1928, 152 houses were torn down, and by 1933 other houses beyond the slum area that were lacking amenities and below health regulation standards were cleared. All that remains of the character of the area are the almshouses in Church Street, which were also in a dilapidated condition but were only saved after a public appeal. The old workers' cottages next to the silk mill at Rookery Road were demolished and replaced with the semi-detached council houses of the Wiggenhall Estate to be occupied by the former tenants of Ballard's Buildings.

Most working-class developments were built on what had largely been farmland, such as the Harebreaks Estate off Gammon's Lane where a thousand houses were built specifically for factory workers. This was Watford's first large-scale public housing development. With the stylistic uniformity of its terraced and semi-detached houses and their front and back gardens, the green open spaces and the symmetrical layout, it followed the model of the contemporary 'garden suburb'. Leavesden, which up until then had been largely an agricultural community, saw the development of several housing estates during the 1930s. The estate at Leavesden Green housed around 1,000 ex-residents from the pre-eighteenth-century core of central Watford to as far as Beechen Grove. They were not particularly happy at having been moved. They had to commute two and a half miles to work, pay 7s rent and there was no school. The latter was remedied with the building of the Leggatts Way School. To the south of the town there were municipal developments too, around Oxhey in Eastbury Road and Thorpe Crescent and southeast by Water Lane.

Most people at this time lived in either private or council rented accommodation, but there were private developments for sale for the growing middle class. The reports in the *Watford Observer* show that for those who could afford it, the 1930s saw something of a building boom. There were the exclusive detached residences close to the town, built on the land purchased from the Cassiobury estate in 1933, occupied by middle-class families who could afford at least one maid and a house-keeper. Less exclusive houses were built in North Watford, in the Kingswood Estate and in Bushey Mill Lane. The Tudor estate was known for its 'Rice's Remarkable Residences' with prices ranging from £700 to £1,000 and the Bradshaw estate in Bushey Mill Lane for its spacious 'semis'. By the '30s some semis had the luxury of garage space, a sign of changing times. Similar developments took place along Oxhey Avenue towards Watford Heath, and in 1934, 656 houses became available costing from £500 to £1,000 on 62 acres of the Durrants Estate and Parrott's Farm in Croxley Green. Building at Parrott's Farm was interrupted by the war, leaving some houses with only the footings in place.

This spate of development was happening despite the hardships of a poor national economic situation, exemplified by the General Strike of 1926 and the world depression caused by the Wall Street Crash of 1929. The improvement in transport links brought an influx of new industries that augmented or superseded the long established trades. Many of the old firms that had been commandeered for wartime work found the change of reverting to a peacetime economy hard. There was unrest as returning servicemen sought work in a more competitive job market, and many women found themselves surplus to requirements. Unemployment depressed wages and as a result workers in the industrial areas went on strike. The repercussions of the General Strike were largely felt elsewhere, mainly in the north, but railway workers (the railway was a major employer in the town), busmen and members of the print industry came out on strike. During the 1930s, Watford's unemployment rate was below the national average, so it suffered less than elsewhere. Even so, in line with national policy there were local initiatives to create jobs. Watford Council used public building and repair works for that purpose and relief could be obtained by the out of work, but this was dependent on the hated Means Test, which was introduced in 1931. Other initiatives had national implications. In order to retrain unemployed miners and heavy industry workers from the North and Midlands as mechanics and builders, a government training centre was opened in the Delectaland factory in North Watford. This was seen as unfair competition by the local unemployed, who were not in receipt of such support. The resentment exploded into violence in the centre of Watford when, as the *Watford Observer* reported, local youths attacked the ex-miners with truncheons, lead pipes, razors and knuckle-dusters, forcing them to take refuge in the Palace Theatre.

Delectaland was the home of the Watford Manufacturing Company, makers of Dr Tibbles' Cocoa and other confectionary delights at their Victoria Works in Callowland between St Albans Road and Bushey Mill Lane. The company found the change back from war work to their previous more light-hearted incarnation difficult and after only a brief resurgence as its former self, it went bankrupt in 1922. The factory was taken over by British Moulded Hose in 1929. Immediately after the war, the area around Callowland and Bushey Mill Lane that had been taken for munitions factories became available for peacetime use, and new industries began moving into what became known as the Imperial/Colonial Way Industrial Estate. HM No. 1 Munitions Works became split between Penfold Fencing and part of the Co-operative (demolished 1985). In January 1919, the *Watford Observer* reported the government sale of a previous 'projectile factory', HM No. 2, a thirty-three acre site comprising 124,000 square feet of buildings. In 1926, the Greycaine Book Manufacturing Company took over twenty acres of the site that included the wooden buildings of the old Filling Works near Watford North Railway Station with access to its own railway siding connected to the Euston mainline. The old buildings were quickly replaced with sturdier, less flammable structures, an indictment of the previous safety levels. There was a post-war revival for some companies, such as Blyth and Platt, to which the wartime disruption to supplies had caused problems. Production continued at their Cobra works in Bushey, where the brand of polish was made even after the company was bought out by Chiswick Products in 1928.

The continued development of light industry in the town and its environs would play a significant role in the area's prosperity and in the looming war. Successful local companies would soon find themselves in the front line in the country's hour of need. Cox & Co, formerly Cox of Watford, founded in the late 1920s by Roland Wilton Cox, built a brand new Art Deco factory on the bypass. Cox, who had begun by making car accessories for the vehicle manufacturer Rotax, was a pioneer in early windscreen design and tubular automobile seating. After splitting with Rotax, Cox shifted the company's focus to military vehicles and private commissions. Influenced by the 1930s classic Bauhaus designs of the German Thonet company, his early notable orders included 5,000 chairs for Bobby's Department Store in Bournemouth, 2,500 tables for Dreamland, Margate, a series of pieces for the BBC's Broadcasting House (1931-2) and flip-up seating for the Royal Institute of British Architects in 1935. The furniture springs were supplied by the Chiswell Wire Company, founded in 1932 nearby in Sandown Road at the Balmoral Road end of Delectaland.

Some companies would have a more obvious military future. The Watford Electric & Manufacturing Company (WEMCO), based in Whippendell Road since 1911, began concentrating on automatic switchgear during the war and by 1922 they were producing control gears for automatic electric motors, pumps, air compressors and lifts, and control equipment for electric furnaces. During the 1930s the company grew rapidly, developing many patented devices for motor starters. In 1936 it became a public company listed on the London Stock Exchange. Its expertise in switchgear manufacture would be a major component of the aviation industry. One of the newcomers, Scammell Lorries, had begun their production of articulated trucks in 1920 at their old Spitalfields premises. In order to expand, in 1922, they opened a new factory on a green-field site in Tolpits Lane next to West Watford station on the branch line from Watford Junction to Croxley Green, where they developed a series of heavy vehicles and tractors.

Successful as some of these companies were, by the 1920s printing was the biggest industry in Watford. Through constant innovation the town had become the most important printing centre in the world. The merging of the remaining small firms completed the pre-war trend towards consolidation. Ashworth, Meredith & Downer, Geo. Jones Ltd (renamed Menpes Printing and Engraving) whose sizeable works in Whipendell Road was built in 1906, and the Bushey Colour Press, all became part of Sun Engraving. Sun Engraving on Whippendell Road now employed 2,000 staff and produced over twenty-five magazines. The capture of the contract for the *Picture Post* in 1938, which had a circulation of 1.5 million, was enough to offset the competition from its new rival Odhams.

In 1935 the newspaper and magazine publishers Odhams Press set up a vast works (70,000 sq ft floor space and 50,000 sq ft basement), Odhams (Watford) Ltd, on wasteland to the north of the town with the primary object of undertaking high-speed colour photogravure printing. It was a major undertaking that required the sinking of wells, laying on of power and building the infrastructure to take in supplies of paper and ink and for the dispatch of the finished materials worldwide. As the number of employees grew, 1,500 houses were built in response. As the chairman of the company, Julius Elias, Viscount Southwood, noted, this led to auxiliary services being provided for the new community such as 'bakeries, greengrocers' shops, butchers, chemists and schools for the children'. In the autumn of 1936, printing began on periodicals that included *Mickey Mouse*, *Picturegoer*, *Zoo*, *Mother*, *Illustrated*, *Everywoman* and Elias' new colour magazine, *Woman*. So much production was undertaken that work on another factory block began in 1937; it became operational in 1939.

During the 1930s Hertfordshire began to become a major centre for the growing aircraft industry. The opening of the Barnet bypass in 1928 made the flying club of the De Havilland Aircraft Company near Hatfield a more suitable site for their works than at Stag Lane Aerodrome, Edgware. Established in late 1920 by Geoffrey de Havilland, the company had been aviation innovators since their inception and were responsible for a number of important aircraft, including the Moth biplane, which revolutionised general aviation in the 1920s and '30s. The Fox Moth was the first commercial transport able to operate without government subsidy. From 1930 to 1938 their workforce grew from 900 to 4,820.

While aviation went on to play an important role in the future, the growing film industry based around Elstree and Borehamwood would be mothballed in 1939 by the War Office, its success coming after the war. In Bushey, the artist Hubert von Herkomer, who died in 1914, left the beginnings of a nascent homegrown film industry. His studios next to Lululand, his house in

Melbourne Road, were used from 1913 by the Bushey Film Corporation. A.E. Matthews, who had acted in his early films and lived in Little Bushey Lane, bought Herkomer's old equipment and from 1915 the British Actors Film Company, a consortium of prominent stage actors that included Matthews and Leslie Howard, produced a number of silent dramas. The company was never financially sound and in 1923 it was taken over by another short-lived enterprise, Minerva Films, whose directors included A.A. Milne, C. Aubrey Smith and Leslie Howard. After the break-up of Minerva, the studios continued to be let for film production throughout the interwar period, but the house did not fare so well. Lululand fell derelict. It remained largely unoccupied and, due to increasing expense, was almost completely demolished in 1939, with only a remnant of the façade surviving. Early film production had fared better in Borehamwood where it continued under a number of companies during the interwar period. In Elstree, where film production had begun in 1925, Alfred Hitchcock made the first British 'talkie', *Blackmail*, at the Shenley Road studios for British International Pictures.

Outside Watford and the new housing estates, many of the towns and villages were still small. In the 1930s Hemel Hempstead Rural District only had a population of around 10,000. Agricultural life continued seemingly unchanged, but there were already indications of a new kind of farming and food production on the horizon. Ovaltine, the originally Swiss milk-based drink, was a pioneer multinational company, and in 1913 they opened a new British factory at Kings Langley with a workforce of thirteen. The factory expanded rapidly during the interwar period and between 1924 and 1929 the Art Deco style main factory (only the façade remains) was built to house a workforce of 700. Kings Langley was chosen as the surrounding farms could produce many of the ingredients needed to make Ovaltine and there was a ready supply of water and local labour. The factory was conveniently situated next to the Grand Union Canal, where fuel for the boilers was delivered by narrow boat from the Warwickshire coalfield, and the railway line. In 1930 the company purchased the two farms that became the Ovaltine Dairy and Poultry 'model' farms. Here they set the standard for the production of barley, milk and eggs, the main ingredients of the Ovaltine drink. The company vision of quality and healthy, country goodness was symbolised by the Ovaltine Dairy Maid who first appeared on their advertising in the 1920s.

With Watford growing into an enterprising engineering hub, but still set within a rural area not yet fully drawn into the greater London conurbation, the image of the area during the '20s and '30s is of a dynamic community on the cusp of embracing change and a progressive future. But these dreams would be nipped in the bud before they had time to fully materialise by outside forces and events elsewhere.

CHAPTER TWO

A hush over all Europe

What kind of a hush is it? Alas! it is the hush of suspense, and in many lands it is the hush of fear. Listen! ... I think I hear something... the tramp of armies crunching the gravel of the parade-grounds, splashing through rain-soaked fields, the tramp of two million German soldiers and more than a million Italians - "going on maneuvers"...

Speech made by Winston Churchill on 8 August 1939

Throughout the 1930s the prospect of another war in Europe gathered pace. Despite attempts by Britain and France, and the protests of smaller countries and the League of Nations, the threat of Nazi Germany and Fascist Italy grew. With increasing confidence Hitler and Mussolini began flexing their muscles in foreign interventions; first Italy invading Ethiopia (1935) and then Germany helping Franco's fascists in Spain (1936-9). Even as Adolf Hitler, under pretence of 'liberating' and unifying the German speaking peoples, annexed Austria (1938) and then seized Czechoslovakia (1938-9), there was the further threat of Japan, which was invading China (1937-8). In a warning speech to an American audience (quoted above), Winston Churchill makes it clear that by the summer of 1939 the diplomatic efforts of the British Prime Minister, Neville Chamberlain, had failed to deliver 'peace for our time'.

The catastrophe of the Great War left a British nation reluctant to rearm, and it was only in 1935 as the situation worsened that the process began with a limited budget being spent on the air force and navy. Although Britain's main potential antagonists were already identified as Germany and Japan, it was thought that any conflict would be one of 'limited liability' ruling out any need for the reconditioning of the army. But during the slow build up to the declaration of war, events on the continent were already having their effect in Britain. The displacement of peoples under the racial policy of Hitler's Nazi regime began as early as 1933, when he assumed power as Chancellor. From then on Jewish immigrants fleeing persecution began to arrive in Britain in significant numbers (around 40,000 from Austria and Germany and 50,000 from Poland, Italy and Eastern Europe) until visas, introduced in 1938 to limit access, were cancelled on the outbreak of war. In contrast the *Kindertransport* run by volunteer organizations to rescue children was allowed by the government, resulting in their placement in foster homes, hostels, schools and farms. The situation regarding refugees was highlighted in the *Watford Observer* (27 January 1939), when Mrs. K. Freeman responded to the plight of 'the persecuted Jews and Non-Aryans in Germany' by organizing a home for refugee children in Gilling Lodge, Church Road, Watford, supported by the Bishop of St Albans and a fund raised by the Watford Churches. The children ranged from as young as 2 years old to 16, and a matron and staff, including two German women refugees, were to be provided. Mrs Freeman was an ardent campaigner on behalf of Palestinian Christians through her work on the Church of England's Committee for the Care of Non-Aryan Christian Refugees.

'Jewish and Non-Aryan' women refugees from Germany and Austria were already finding domestic employment within Hertfordshire and it was proposed that educated and 'cultured' women, some already with nursing background, expressing a desire to work as nurses should be taken on in the local hospitals. In response to a question in the Mass Observation Survey for March 1939, a female teacher from Watford dismissed any idea of 'Britain for the British' put forward by the British Union of Fascists, arguing that 'our country will eventually benefit by having and using the ability and talents of the Jews, just as we have in the past gained an enormous amount from Flemish weavers, and Huguenot silk, leather and wood workers.' But with the declaration of war the status of German nationals turned from 'Alien' to 'enemy Alien'. Then, in 1940, Churchill ordered that the Aliens should be interned and in a strange moment of reversal Jewish refugees from the area found themselves sleeping on mattresses in Watford's Drill Hall on their way to the internment camps.

Despite Chamberlain's best efforts, the general mood was that war was imminent, and precautions were already under discussion within local bodies. At the Watford School managers meeting in January the provision of bombproof shelters was put forward by Alderman R.J. Bridger who argued that it would be too late if it was left until the outbreak of hostilities, putting the safety of the 7,000 children under their care at risk. The official thinking after the last war was that bombing would play a significant role in any future conflict. Following the then prime minister Stanley Baldwin's initiative in September 1935, entitled 'Air Raid Precautions (ARP)', circulated to local authorities to encourage making plans for the protection of the populace, Hertfordshire County Council set up its ARP Committee. Watford followed suit the following year and an inspection of civil defences was held. To chivvy up slow moving councils the Air Raid Wardens' Service was created in April 1937, and by September the following year the membership reached 700,000. In Watford the ARP took over Watford Field House, once the residence of the council's surveyor and engineer Dennis Waterhouse. By the summer of 1938 matters were becoming serious when the government drew up an evacuation scheme for women and children. In Hertfordshire, Watford Municipal

Borough, Bushey, Cheshunt and East Barnet Urban Districts and Barnet Rural District, which bordered on to Greater London, were declared neutral zones, meaning that there were no plans for evacuation, but neither would evacuees move in. Watford was, however, a 'distributing centre' from where children travelling out from London could be transferred by rail to rural areas.

In September, international tensions were stretched to the limit. When Hitler threatened to forcibly 'liberate' the Sudetenland, the German-speaking area of Czechoslovakia, emergency talks were held in Munich to avert all-out war (the Munich Crisis). With the situation teetering on the brink, in scenes reminiscent of the previous conflict, trenches were dug in Cassiobury Park, and then as events vacillated to and fro, the council debated whether to fill them in again. To a background of reports in the *Watford Observer* that the Crisis was causing panic, the Mayor of Watford entreated the local community to stay calm, stressing that war was not inevitable; then he arranged for 50,000 gas masks to be assembled in ten hours. The mayor followed government instructions to utilize local companies and 600 workers from four laundries (the Model, Watford Steam, Millars and Silverdale) and the Sun Engraving Works were rushed into assembling the masks. In the event gas masks were not issued to civilians until 1939, and when they were they proved both unpopular and in the end unnecessary. Children, who had to practise putting them on at school, were reluctant to use them because they were uncomfortable to wear and had an off-putting smell of rubber.

On 30 September Chamberlain returned to London famously waving his piece of paper in the belief that he had done a deal with Hitler that would secure 'peace for our time'. The price was leaving the door open for German troops to march triumphantly into Czechoslovakia. As Churchill foresaw in a letter to Lloyd George in August, 'England has been offered a choice between war and shame. She has chosen shame, and will get war.' Chamberlain's policy of 'appeasement' was in part guided by the state of the nation's finances. The austerity years of the Great Depression had exacerbated the huge expense of the First World War and this had left the public purse seriously depleted. As a consequence the British Armed Forces were in a sad state due to the lack of funds available to upgrade their equipment. In reality the Munich Agreement had done nothing to relieve the tense international situation and now it was a race against time to prepare for the inevitable outcome of Nazi militarism. This new reality was put to the test in early February 1939, when the ARP in Watford Rural District took part in night exercises in 'wartime conditions' that included the Fire Brigade, Red Cross, St John's Ambulance and 1,000 volunteers. Ten warning sirens were set off, phone lines disabled and casualty centres set up over a large area covering Bushey in the south, Radlett in the east, Sarratt and Abbots Langley in the north and Rickmansworth in the west.

The next step was a government drive to recruit volunteers for the Territorial Army and the Civil Defence. In response, a committee was set up for Hertfordshire (it met in London) under Viscount Hampden. Thomas Brand, the 3rd Viscount, had served as an officer with the 1st Battalion of the Hertfordshire Regiment on the Western Front in the first war and from 1915 he succeeded the Earl of Clarendon as Lord Lieutenant of the county. An area of immediate recruiting concern was the lack of volunteers in Watford, St Albans, Hitchin and Hertford for the Women's Auxiliary Service. In March 1939, Prague fell to the Nazis. In response, the government finally abandoned its budget constraints on the military and conscription began in April, initially limited to training 20 to 22-year-old unmarried men to act as reservists for the regular army; and once again Clarendon Hall, in a replay of 1914, was pressed into military use. As mobilization began, Lady Gertrude Denham, a veteran of the organization of the Women's Land Army during the last war, realized that one crucial battle to come might be fought on the fields of Britain. She had begun petitioning the government in late 1938, arguing that to maintain the provision of food an alternative workforce would have to be recruited to replace the men taken from the countryside. Although farming was to be a reserved occupation, this would only apply to the farmer, not to labourers. In June 1939, the Women's Land Army (WLA) was reintroduced to fill the gap under the honorary leadership of Lady Denham, but under the control of the Ministry of Agriculture and Fisheries. Commonly referred to as Land Girls, the members were to play a vital role in the war effort. At first membership was voluntary but later conscription was introduced. The first intake of women in Hertfordshire numbered 65; by 1943 the figure would rise to over 2,100.

With little prospect of peace, preparations began to be made for the impact of war on the local population. Watford Council arranged for the setting up of communal street air-raid shelters and the distribution of family Morrison shelters for inside the home. Morrison shelters were similar to hiding from falling masonry under a very robust table. The outdoor corrugated steel Anderson shelters were partly sunk into the garden. As a further precaution households were advised to put brown paper sticky tape latticed across window glass to prevent it from shattering. On 8 July, Watford Borough tested its air-raid sirens situated in Chilcott Avenue, Greenwood Drive, Tudor Avenue, Langley Way and Cardiff Road, the latter of which came to be affectionately known as 'Moaning Minnie'.

In June 1939 with the passing of the Military Training Act made all men aged 20-21 liable for call-up for four years military service as 'Militiamen'. This was followed by the recall of Parliament on 24 August and the passing of the Emergency Powers (Defence) Act that enabled the government to call up army reservists and civil defence workers. Volunteers of ex-servicemen were sent to guard vulnerable points and on 30 August the fleet was put on war stations. The army began its official mobilization on Friday, 1 September, when German forces marched into Poland. The next day civil defence personnel were mobilized, the first nationwide nightly 'blackout' introduced, and the plans for the evacuation of children and nursing and expectant mothers from London and other possible targets prepared for action. On Sunday, after Hitler ignored Chamberlain's ultimatum to withdraw from Poland by 11 pm, Britain and France declared war on Germany.

CHAPTER THREE

Call to Arms

For the next five years much of Britain would become a militarised zone, particularly in the south. Men and women in uniform would be everywhere and many aspects of life would be geared to the needs of the military. The four railway companies were joined together becoming in effect one company to coordinate and facilitate movement of troops and supplies and factories were turned to producing armaments and munitions. Even those not directly involved in front line soldiering could soon find themselves in uniform, and there were other less obvious activities going on below the surface out of the public eye.

In the first weeks there was no repeat of the jingoistic fervour that had greeted the declaration of war in August 1914, more a resigned acceptance of the inevitable. In March the Territorial Army had been brought up to a war footing, doubling up the number of field units, followed by the introduction of limited conscription in April. Once again would-be soldiers were to be seen reporting to the Drill Hall (Clarendon Hall) in Watford, and in May a 'Mock Air Attack' was put on in Cassiobury Park accompanied by a procession and display to encourage recruitment. So when war finally came there was almost a national sense of relief. At last the waiting was over and Hitler's aggression could be confronted. Immediately, National Service was implemented, with full conscription for men aged between 18 and 41. Each arm of the three forces had its own Regular and Territorial regiments and reservists, plus auxiliaries. Reservists and volunteers had the luxury of choosing which regiment to serve in, whereas those called up could only chose between the army, navy and air force. Large buildings were requisitioned. Those within parkland were ideal; buildings like the nineteenth-century Kytes House, in what was still countryside on the edge of Garston, which was procured by the army. The military needed room and Hertfordshire's ample rural spaces had an established tradition of serving their needs. In the latter years of the war the Chiltern Hills would provide the location for exercises and hiding regiments of armoured vehicles.

Not everyone was required to do national service. Soldiers had to be physically fit and not employed in a 'reserved occupation', a job deemed essential to the national interest. Other exemptions could be made. The experiences of the last war had changed attitudes and a somewhat softer approach was taken to conscientious objectors. Although there had been a significant peace movement during the interwar period, especially amongst those with Leftist or progressive political leanings, once Hitler's intentions became clear and war began, the perceived justice of the cause meant dissent largely melted away. Fascists opposing the war, and whose politics aligned them with Germany, were given short shrift and sent to prison. Pacifist organisations did continue, and some objectors still faced prison, but those with religious convictions, such as Quakers and Seventh Day Adventists, who two decades earlier had suffered for their beliefs, were treated with better understanding. Previously, 130 Adventist men, many of them based around the Church headquarters at Stanborough Park in Watford, had been imprisoned. This time they, like other objectors, were required to appear before a tribunal, and if successful were assigned to useful jobs or deployed in the Non-Combatant Corps or the Royal Army Medical Corps; this might mean work on a farm or in a hospital. Some conscientious objectors, however, volunteered for more dangerous non-combatant activities, including bomb disposal. Despite the official more enlightened approach there was still a general local antagonism to 'conchies', and Watford Council refused to employ them. In Kings Langley residents expressed their disgust that the significant number of local members of the Baptist Pacifist Union was a slur against the village. When the air raids began, feelings became heightened and a pacifist stance was harder to maintain. Such lingering ill feeling was enough to compel many conscientious objectors to move away from the area after the war.

Medical staff, the police, engineers and skilled workers were exempted from call-up, but the requirements were fluid – the military needed doctors and engineers too – and increasing numbers of women were moved into men's jobs. Although teaching was a reserved occupation, it only applied to those over 25 and many schools began to suffer from a lack of able-bodied male teachers. One such teacher was Vivian Cox, who taught English and Drama at Aldenham School. As a naval voluntary reservist he went on to serve at the heart of the government's strategic decision-making. In 1940 he was picked to work in the Admiralty War Room and went on to design the floating map room for Winston Churchill aboard the battleship *Duke of York* and a similar one for President Roosevelt. After the war he became a well-known producer at Pinewood Studios.

More generally, schools provided a ready pathway into military recruitment for the pupils. A well-established tradition of cadet corps existed in a number of local schools and these would have affiliations to volunteer battalions and Territorial reserves. Officer Training Corps (OTCs) already in existence at St Albans School and Aldenham School were redesignated as Junior Training Corps in 1940. The Hertfordshire Cadets, which were affiliated to the Hertfordshire Regiment, had units in a number of towns (including St Albans, Hatfield and Watford) and Hertfordshire schools. After a lapse during the interwar period, the Watford Grammar School Cadets were reformed in 1942 and affiliated to the Hertfordshire Regiment and then the Hertfordshire Yeomanry. At the Royal Masonic School in Bushey the Cadets were affiliated to the Hertfordshire Regiment and the London Rifles. The Army Cadet Force was then expanded in 1942 so that the Hertfordshire Regiment's Cadet Battalions had companies in Victoria Boys School and Leggatts Way School in Watford, Durrant's Senior School in Croxley Green, and detachments in Garston, Borehamwood, Radlett, St Albans, London Colney, Hemel Hempstead, Kings Langley, Bovingdon and Abbots Langley.

It was natural for many of the recruits to join local regiments. The Bedfordshire and Hertfordshire Regiment, renamed in 1919 to include Hertfordshire in recognition of the contribution of the men from the county in the First World War, had both regular and Territorial battalions. The 1st Battalion were based in the Middle East in 1938 and were then posted to India in 1942. They saw action during the Burma campaign (1944) with the Chindits where they suffered such heavy casualties they took no further part in the war. The 2nd Battalion was posted to France as part of the ill-fated British Expeditionary Force, and subsequently evacuated from Dunkirk. In 1941 they were posted to North Africa and saw action during the invasion of Italy (1944) and the liberation of Greece (1944-5). After home defence duties the 5th Battalion was posted to Malaya in 1942 where it participated in the disastrous surrender of Singapore to the Japanese. As local war memorials testify many men from the region serving in these regiments lost their lives in foreign fields. Those of the 5th, if they did not die first, suffered incarceration for the duration of the war in the notorious Japanese prison and labour camps.

The Hertfordshire Regiment, on the other hand, was a purely Territorial regiment. TA reservists were mobilized as far as possible from their own counties, but in time their local character was diluted with reinforcements from other counties. The 1st Battalion of the regiment covered the north and east of the county, while the 2nd Battalion covered the south and west with its headquarters in Watford. HQ Company was based there, apart from one platoon in Rickmansworth, and the other four companies spread, with No. 1 at St Albans, No. 2 at Hemel Hempstead and Nos. 3 and 4 at Berkhamsted, minus two platoons each based at Tring. The Hertfordshire Regiment was combined with the 6th Battalion of the Bedford and Hertfordshire Regiment to form the 162 Infantry Brigade of 54th (East Anglian) Division deployed in a counter-invasion role. This meant postings around the east coast until April 1940, then Northumberland until March 1941, and finally various parts of the southern counties. The Brigade was split up in April 1943 when the 1st Battalion was sent oversees to Gibraltar, and then on to Italy. In August the 2nd Battalion became part of the combined operations of the D-Day landings, forming the basis of 9 Beach Group that landed at Ver-sur-Mer, Normandy. The battalion was dispersed in 1944 to provide reinforcements for other forward troops.

With the reorganisation of the Territorial Army after the First World War, the Hertfordshire Yeomanry was transformed from a cavalry unit to become part of the Royal Artillery. Split into two regiments, the 86th (East Anglian) (Hertfordshire Yeomanry) Field Regiment was based in the south of the county at St Albans and Hertford, and the 135th in the north at Hitchin and Northampton. In 1939 the old pre-war Watford Field Battery became an anti-aircraft brigade. On mobilization the regiment mustered 1,100 men. Until 1942, the 86th was used in an anti-invasion role, first in East Anglia, then in Northumberland. In 1944 it was attached to the British Second Army, participating in the D-Day landings and the liberation of occupied Europe, becoming part of the army of occupation in Germany until 1946. The 79th (Hertfordshire Yeomanry) Heavy Anti-Aircraft Regiment had its headquarters and two batteries at Watford with a third recruited at Welwyn Garden City. As war became imminent the Territorial anti-aircraft units were mobilized in August and the regiment was put on war stations at various airfields around the Home Counties and East Anglia, finally seeing action protecting Harwich and Felixstowe before being shipped to France. Back in England in 1940, the regiment was constantly in action in the north-west and south Wales before being posted to North Africa in 1943 and Italy in 1944.

For women there was the option of the Auxiliary Territorial Service. The ATS had been in existence for a year by the outbreak of war. In the early phase the volunteers of the ATS were attached to established Territorial units as cooks, clerks, storekeepers, drivers and telephonists, but in time their roles were expanded and they were given more responsibility, acting as military support: radar operators, anti-aircraft gun crew, searchlight operators and military police. In Watford, the 2nd Hertfordshire Company ATS was affiliated to the 79th Anti-Aircraft Regiment, and the 3rd Hertfordshire Company to the 1st Battalion Hertfordshire Regiment in St Albans. In 1941, unmarried women between 20 and 30 were called up to join one of the auxiliary services attached to the army, navy or air force, the Women's Voluntary Service (WVS) or the Land Army. The seriousness of the contribution of the ATS is borne out by two graves, one in Watford Cemetery and the other in North Watford Cemetery, of volunteers who lost their lives on active service.

Each of the seven sons of Mrs T. Nicholls from Mill End, Watford, chose or was enlisted in different branches of the military. William and Thomas volunteered for the Royal Engineers, John joined the Herts and Beds and Eric and Arthur served in India, Arthur in the RAF. The last two served in Sicily with the RE and the Royal Army Service Corps. Mrs Nicholls was lucky, all survived. In the meantime, four of her six daughters were involved in war work. (Another Royal Engineer was Thomas Blackwell from Chipperfield who earned the George Medal and the MBE (Military) for doing the harrowing job of bomb disposal on Malta).

For those not suitable for full-time military duty there were other opportunities to serve. The Observer Corps (designated Royal in 1941), mobilized a week before the outbreak of war, was made up of part-time volunteers. The corps was part of southern England's anti-aircraft defences and it had fifteen observation posts in Hertfordshire. Its role was to supplement the capability of coastal radar in the early warning of approaching enemy aircraft by tracking their course inland and giving added information such as the type, course, height and speed of the aircraft. The corps headquarters was at RAF Bentley Priory near Bushey Heath, and command posts and observation centres in Hertfordshire were occupied continuously for the duration of the war. The protection of London, most of the Home Counties north of the Thames and parts of Surrey and Kent fell to 17th Group who had their HQ in Watford, and during the Battle of Britain their resources were pushed to the limit. Initially the operations room was a makeshift affair above Watford Post Office in Market Street run by the librarian George Bolton, before it moved in August 1943 to a purpose-built blockhouse in Cassiobury Drive with a two-storey control room. Film of the Observer Corps at work in their Watford operations room shot by Pathé News in 1952 exists and can be accessed on the internet. It is thought that the roof of the newly built block in The Parade (nos 58-68) was one of the lookout points for spotting enemy planes. Other high points, such as the towers of St Peter's Church (reputedly the highest and coldest point in Hertfordshire) and the Masonic School in Bushey and Abbots Langley Church, and factory roofs, such as WEMCO's in Whippendell Road, were used; and not to be deterred by lack of elevation Cox and Co in Watford erected their own 60ft spotting tower in Hartspring Lane. The landmark 46m-tall tower of Shenley Hospital on top of Shenley Ridge, visible for about three miles in each direction, offered an ideal location for a fire-watch post and military radiocommunications surveillance.

The Senior Service and the Air Force

Living in land-locked Hertfordshire was no barrier to those feeling the call of the sea and local men signed up as reservists in the Royal Navy (RNR). Men with sailing experience could become officers in the Royal Navy Voluntary Reserve. Women too could serve in the navy or air force in the Women's Royal Navy Service (WRNS, popularly the Wrens) or in the Women's Auxiliary Air Force (WAAF). The Wrens were employed in shore based activities and code breaking. Local reservists in the navy or air force served, and gave their lives, in far-flung locations as the information on war memorials shows. For those at sea, like Sub-Lieutenant Michael Eden of Abbots Langley who went down with HMS *Ark Royal* when it was torpedoed in November 1941, there would be no memorial except their name.

The romance of flight had grown in appeal between the wars and there were increasing numbers of young enthusiasts and local flying clubs, ideal recruiting grounds for the Royal Air Force Reserve (RAFR). The RAF had its own Territorial formations known as the Royal Auxiliary Air Force (RAAF), and in 1936 part of it formed the Royal Air Force Voluntary Reserve (RAFVR). The duties of the women of the WAAF were far ranging and included working in catering, meteorology, transport, telephony and telegraphy, on aircraft maintenance, codes and ciphers, in the Intelligence, Security and Operation Rooms, and some even as pilots delivering aircraft to active airfields. At Fighter Command HQ at Bentley Priory they were given the responsibility of operating and interpreting the radar information that provided the early warning of enemy attack. The women were paid two thirds less than the men and unless they were lucky enough to own a bicycle, for entertainment they might have to walk the four miles into Watford and back to go to the cinema. When war broke out the Air Ministry employed the RAFVR as the principal means for aircrew entry and by 1941 more than half of the RAF bomber crews were recruited from their ranks. The service had close links with the Air Defence Cadet Corps (ADCC), formed in 1938, and members would help in training the Cadets. ADCC No 2 Squadron was based in Watford.

The impact on a local community of their loved ones serving in the forces is borne out by the nineteen RAF volunteer reservists listed on the Christ Church War Memorial in North Watford. Of these, Sergeant Frank Walter was lost missing in action during an attack on Kiel docks in 1940 and similarly Pilot Officer Arthur Schofield's Halifax went missing over Denmark in 1943. The increase in bomber activity during 1944 is reflected in an increased number of losses: Sergeant (Flight Engineer) Dennis Aird's Halifax, shot down over Poland; Flight Sergeant Kenneth Horne's Wellington bomber, missing on a raid on Bohlen in Germany; Warrant Officer Michael Medcalf's Halifax bomber, shot down over Denmark. Went missing were the Lancaster bombers of Sergeant Jack Lea (in support of the D-Day landings), Flying Officer Philip Rowe DFC (over France) and Sergeant Frederick Sloane (over Germany). Fighter pilots also served and died abroad, Pilot Officer Alex Wainwright from St Albans died in North Africa in 1941 flying Hurricanes for 72 Squadron and in the Far East, Flight Lieutenant John Luing's Beaufighter was shot down and he was taken prisoner and died in Rangoon jail. The poignancy of the human story behind such bald statements is brought home by the story of Pilot Officer Bernard Baldwin, 158 Squadron, from Apsley who was killed in May 1944 flying his Halifax bomber over Aachen. He had just passed his final interview for a commission as a flying officer. In the *Watford Observer* report his mother revealed that 'He had striven so hard to become an officer' and that there was £7 in the post that she had sent him to buy whatever he needed when he received his promotion the following Saturday. His medals were awarded posthumously.

Eighteen-year old Flying Officer Leslie Thomas Manser, an ex-pupil of Aldenham School from Radlett, joined the RAF in 1940. On a bombing mission over Cologne in 1942 his Avro Manchester was hit and bound to crash. Ordering his crew to bail out he stayed at the controls to save them. He was awarded a posthumous VC.

Thankfully, not all the stories ended sadly. Robert Norman Bateson, who was educated at Watford Boys Grammar, had a distinguished RAF career. He joined the RAF in 1936 and went on to achieve the rank of Air Vice Marshal, winning numerous decorations on the way. Bateson gained notoriety for his exploits in leading a series of daring low-level precision bombing attacks, the success of which earned him the nickname 'Pinpoint'. The targets were the Gestapo headquarters in The Hague, Copenhagen (Operation Carthage) and Odense for which he earned the DFC and DSO and bar. In April 1944 the Mosquitoes of No. 613 Squadron under his command destroyed the Gestapo building in The Hague, an exploit for which he received the additional acknowledgement of a Dutch Distinguished Flying Cross personally presented to him by Prince Bernhard of the Netherlands. The citation for the Bar to his DSO read:

> *In March, 1945, Group Captain Bateson led a large formation of aircraft in an attack on the headquarters of the German Gestapo in Copenhagen. The operation called for the highest standard of skill as the target was small and well defended. Nevertheless, the attack was pressed home with a determination and accuracy which ensured success. In April 1945, this officer led his squadrons in an attack against a similar target at Odense. In spite of opposition from the ground defences the attack was vigorously and accurately pressed home. By his brilliant leadership, Group Captain Bateson played an important part in the success of these notable sorties.*

Colin Weall Coulthard, another former pupil of Watford Boys, studied aeronautical engineering at the de Havilland engineering school in Hatfield, before becoming a Spitfire pilot in 1939 and flying missions over Malta and Italy. After the war he stayed in the air force, rising to the rank of air commodore, and then transferred to the Ministry of Defence. Leslie Bonnet, who had stood as Liberal candidate for Watford in the 1920s, joined the Balloon Command in 1938, the only route into the military for someone aged 36. After various commands around London during the Battle of Britain he was promoted to Wing Commander in 1942 and sent to China to train the Chinese Air Force. For his services he was awarded the rare Order of the Cloud and Banner with special rosette for his services to China. After the war he became a writer. Flight Lieutenant Peter Cleaver from Oxhey, who was awarded the DFC, became a test pilot at Farnborough in 1945 and Charles Rivington from Chipperfield rose to the rank of Squadron Leader.

Mosquito flying over Copenhagen during Operation Carthage (public domain)

Wall Hall and the War Office Selection Board

The need to quickly recruit the numbers to match the enemy's military superiority was only the first step. British forces were sadly lacking in equipment. The Nazis had spent their time in power in Germany developing a highly efficient and well-trained military machine suited to the technical developments of mechanized warfare, but it soon became apparent that the British army had not kept pace. The failure to counter the German *Blitzkrieg* and the build up to the disaster of Dunkirk also exposed the lack of men and leaders ready for the demands of modern warfare. With the best recruits already cherry-picked by the navy and RAF, the army was in a conservative rut where advancement was held back by the outmoded ideas of an old-fashioned public school officer elite. In consequence there was a small pool of effective candidates for promotion. By late in 1941, the increased demand for suitable officers meant the situation was no longer tenable resulting in a crisis in officer selection. It was finally decided that the old amateurish methods had to be replaced with new techniques and the War Office Selection Board

(WOSB), based in Edinburgh, was set up to address the problem. It was proposed that specialists in the field of psychiatry and psychology, many from the Tavistock Clinic (later Institute) in London, would work on replacing the 'old school tie' with a new approach using in-depth interviews and IQ tests. Wall Hall in Aldenham was chosen as the co-ordination centre for the work that was carried out in a number of locations.

The wealthy anglophile American banker John Pierpont Morgan Junior had purchased Wall Hall in 1910. In 1939 he returned to America (where he died in 1943), leaving the estate, with a military Red Cross hospital at Church Farm, in the hands of the American Ambassador, Joseph Kennedy, father of the future US President, John F. Kennedy. When, in 1940, Joseph Kennedy was pressured to resign his post and return home after publicly endorsing a policy of appeasement with Hitler, the house was left empty until it was taken over by the War Office in 1942 to become the WOSB's Control and Development Centre. The Tavistock group referred to Wall Hall as 'Valhalla' (the Norse god Odin's hall for those slain in combat), reflecting their fear that they did not have the control to fully test their work and that it might be sidelined. Wall Hall was only used to develop selection methods, not in actual recruitment, and the site was not guarded, presumably because the work carried out by the group was one the few wartime projects that was not secret. If, as has been suggested, Wall Hall was also used to train special agents to work with Resistance groups in Belgium and Holland, this may have been some form of elaborate double bluff. At the end of 1942 the dissatisfaction of the clinical staff led to a change of name, to the Research and Training Centre, and relocation to Hampstead. Although there was scepticism as to the effectiveness of the new methods, even from Winston Churchill, the psychological approach achieved results and once implemented the calibre of officer was significantly improved. The other services soon followed the army's example and after the war a number of institutions copied the Tavistock group's methods, notably the Civil Service, the Treasury and Unilever.

The Home Guard

In the first phase of the conflict the war may have seemed far away across the Channel, but there was a general realisation that Britain was under-prepared. The threat of invasion was therefore a realistic possibility. As ever on the front foot, Churchill, as First Lord of the Admiralty, urged the forming of a home defence force recruited from those ineligible for call-up to the forces. Local initiatives only led to ill-organised and poorly resourced militias being formed, but with the fall of Belgium and France, and the BEF's retreat from Dunkirk in May 1940, the increased urgency of the situation meant serious action had to be taken. In a radio broadcast, the War Secretary, Anthony Eden, called for men aged from 17 to 65 to volunteer at their local police station for the Local Defence Volunteers. There was an enthusiastic response and by the next day a quarter of a million had signed up; within six weeks the number rose to 1.5 million. The initial militias had only been given a subsidiary role, with resulting poor morale. At first they had no uniforms or weapons. Churchill, who was now prime minister, wanted the LDV to be given an active part in any disruption of an enemy invasion force. This meant reorganisation, better equipment and training, the manning of defences and formation of guerrilla units, and a change of name – the Home Guard. Although, as in the TV series *Dad's Army*, the CO of the Garston Platoon was a bank manager with no military experience, leadership was usually provided by First World War veterans and many of the training officers had fought with the International Brigades against the Fascists during the Spanish Civil War where they had become adept at guerrilla warfare.

Jimmy Perry, co-writer of *Dad's Army* with David Croft, joined the newly created Watford Home Guard as a 16-year-old after his family had moved there from Hammersmith. Perry claimed that *Dad's Army* was based on reality. But although there was a very elderly lance corporal who had fought at Omdurman (1898), on whom the character of Jones was based, his colleagues were generally not as old or inept. Perry later revealed that his unit was largely made up of recruits around his own age who were waiting to be called up, and due to Major Strong, a 'seasoned guerrilla fighter' who had seen action in Spain, they evolved into 'a very efficient guerrilla force'. The major's concern for their welfare included giving them lectures on social justice. While not doing his bit in the Home Guard, Perry was working in a munitions factory. He found time to reveal where his future lay when he did a 'turn' at the Gaumont Cinema, but his career in comedy would have to wait a while before it was realized; two years later he was serving with the Royal Artillery, a journey that would take him to Burma.

After its formation, the Hertfordshire LDV grew so rapidly that the organisation had to be rationalised after two months' existence into seven battalions. Then the 6th Battalion in Watford proved so unwieldy it too was split into four (6, 8, 9 and 10th) known as the Watford Group. The Watford Group covered Croxley Green, Rickmansworth, Kings Langley, Garston, Bricket Wood and Abbots Langley. In 1941, owing to Watford's proximity to London, the 6th Battalion, which had been formed by Colonel W.H. Briggs, the chairman of Benskins, was placed under the command of London District and the administration of the Middlesex Territorial Army Association. Units within factories were formed into Companies. 30 Company of 9th Battalion (HQ in Garston) covered the North Watford Factories and 19 Company at the De Havilland Aircraft Company in Hatfield, were part of the 4th Battalion based at Welwyn. 10th Battalion HQ was at the junction of St Albans Road and Langley Road in Watford. Lewis Jones, a veteran of the First World War, and his son, who was under age for the army, joined 'B' Company and were

Home Guard soldier not deterred by being without a rifle carrying a homemade pike on Stanmore Common (Bushey Museum)

Home Guard looking more military marching down Watford Bypass (Bushey Museum)

Home Guard despatch riders with motorbikes on parade shows the improvement in equipment (Bushey Museum)

immediately supplied with army fatigues and First World War Canadian rifles. In peacetime, Lewis was a well-known textile designer at Silver Studios in London, but now he was employed in war work at WEMCO. In time the battalion's weapons were upgraded, and as a good shot, he was given a Lewis Gun which he kept with its drum magazines at home in his bedroom wardrobe. When called to action, his job was to take up position in the public house on the railway bridge on the St Albans Road next to the footpath leading to Watford Junction Station.

The GPO, London Transport, the railway companies and other public utilities and large employers had their own Home Guard units. As early as 1936, at John Dickinsons & Co an ARP Committee had been formed and money allocated for the building of air raid shelters at many of the mills. Paper combined with the chemicals stored at their mills meant a potentially highly combustible situation that had to be taken seriously and rotas of fire-watching duties were established. Croxley Mill formed their own Home Guard and at Apsley Mill the buildings were painted with camouflage designs and its Home Guard given the task of manning the anti-aircraft guns. Workers at Sun Engravers volunteered for the Anti-Gas Brigade and women workers for the ARP (Air Wardens) First Aid Party, the Red Cross and St John's Ambulance. Further expansions and reorganisations of the Home Guard followed. As supplies increased, mobile reserve companies were formed, with anti-tank, machine gun and light artillery capabilities, all mounted on requisitioned civilian transport. Anti-aircraft units armed with heavy machine guns were attached to the new 13th Battalion protecting the De Havilland factories at Leavesden and Hatfield. Because of its proximity to the airfield and military plane factory at Leavesden, the Russell's Estate off Hempstead Road was used as a base for a searchlight unit coordinated with the anti-aircraft batteries and fighter squadrons that protected the site from nighttime bombing raids. The Home Guard also participated in the troop training and anti-tank manoeuvres that took advantage of the estate's extensive grounds. Once the bombs had fallen around the targeted factories in Watford, Garston and Hatfield, the Home Guard auxiliary bomb disposal units that were attached to the relevant battalions would be called upon. A unit of the LDV had been formed at The Grove, which was occupied by the Midland & Scottish Railway. When this was developed into a Home Guard unit it had become fairly large with a remit to give twenty-four hour protection to an area that included The Grove and the surrounding roads and railway installations. In order that patrols could be sent out through the night, a Guard Room and dormitory block were provided in the stable buildings. There was also a .22 rifle range, the main benefit of which appears to have been in reducing the local rat population. Fortunately the unit was later issued with .303 rifles and live ammunition.

'Mum's Army' and the Women's Home Defence Corps

The government was resistant to women joining the LDV, but on the ground local commanders accepted women volunteers. Typically, these unofficial members acted in auxiliary capacities, as secretaries, drivers, and in catering roles, but many women in Watford also managed to receive weapons training. Others were content to provide support services through membership in the Women's Voluntary Service. It took until April 1943 for women to be formally enrolled in the Home Guard. Known as Women's Home Guard Auxiliaries, despite their previous efforts they were still not permitted officially to carry weapons, let alone train with them. The young Jimmy Perry must have been aware of this reluctance to accept female volunteers into the Home Guard, as an episode of *Dad's Army*, entitled *Mum's Army* (1970), concerns Captain Mainwaring's disastrous attempt, in comic terms, to enroll women. To circumvent this official stubbornness women formed their own 'illegal' groups under the leadership of the Labour MP Edith Summerskill. By December 1940 these groups had coalesced under the banner of the Women's Home Defence Corps. The women of the WHD, which claimed 30,000 members in April 1943, undertook rifle training and often practised on shooting ranges with local Home Guard units.

Home Defence

One of the first tasks the Watford Home Guard were put to was in helping in the construction of defensive works such as the guard post built on some waste ground by the Watford Bypass about a half mile from Edgware. Such defences were not necessarily built to protect Watford itself, but part of a larger scheme. After the retreat from Dunkirk, the job of organizing Home Defence was given to Field Marshal Edmund Ironside, who took in hand the pressing need to rebuild and rearm the forces and to protect the country from the expected German invasion. First in line of fire was Kent, only thirty miles from France, so naturally a priority, but as the German invasion plans were not known, the whole south coast had to be fortified just in case. Once an invasion force landed all effort would be put into delaying its progress. A series of roadblocks manned by the Home Guard would be set up where enemy armoured vehicles would have to negotiate crossroads and narrow sections of the route. To protect London and the industrial heartland, Ironside planned a national network of 'Stop Lines' made up of static or hard defences, such as pillboxes and tank traps, to give time for mobile troops to respond. The longest stretch, known as the GHQ Line, was from the West Country to the Thames and from Essex to Edinburgh. Particularly strong defences were built along the route from the coast to the capital, but London also had a series of defensive rings constructed through the Home Counties. The concentric rings of anti-tank defences and pillboxes were the London Inner Keep, London Stop

Line Inner (Line C), London Stop Line Central (Line B) and the strongest, the London Stop Line Outer (Line A), which ran through open countryside and was the most developed. Ironside's plan had its critics, who thought he had gone 'pillbox mad', and it was soon abandoned on the grounds that it tied too many troops down in construction work. Instead Churchill adopted the plan of General Alan Brooke, commander of Southern Command, to form mobile reserves to strike directly at the enemy beachheads. Ironside's Outer Ring completely encircled London. It made the most of natural barriers, such as rivers, complemented by artificial ditches 20 feet or more wide and 12 feet deep, tank traps and of course pillboxes. Features such as the trenches dug on Chorleywood Common, on the school playing field in Abbots Langley and at Langleybury Park and the rows of poles connected by wires erected across open land to fend off enemy gliders have disappeared, but some of the more substantial works still survive today. The northern section uses a route similar to that of the M25. Pillboxes and defences can be seen that sandwich Watford to the north and south. At Hunton Bridge, west of Leavesden, a square pillbox

Type 22 pillbox by the roadside at Patchetts Green, near Letchmore Heath. The rough roof surface was a form of camouflage intended to break its outline (Mike Dyer)

Berry Grove pillbox (Mike Dyer)

sits on the west side of Gipsy Lane, to the north of the bridge over the West Coast Main Line north of Watford Tunnels. In a field near Fortunes Farm in Abbots Langley there is an example of the hexagonal type. South of Watford and to the east of the M1, the defensive ring follows the River Colne, and there are a number of pillboxes linking Bushey, Letchmore Heath, Radlett and Shenley. The route then passes on by way of Potters Bar, Cuffley, Nazeing and south through Epping Forest, Loughton and Chigwell.

The pillbox at Potters Bar Golf Course was augmented by an anti-tank ditch, and to the north at Brookmans Park, perhaps purposely near the BBC's regional Transmitting Station, there can still be seen the well-preserved remains of a spigot mortar emplacement. The three-man gun crew operated the mortar mounted on a stainless steel pin set in a concrete base behind a protective concrete embrasure. West from the M1 and over the A41, the route of the ring is picked up again by the concrete octagonal pillbox close to the River Colne at Berry Grove Lane, Bushey, and protecting the main line to Euston there is a pillbox nestling under Bushey Arches, one at Bushey Station between platforms 2 and 3 and another along Pinner Road. Further pillboxes along the Colne defended the south of the town from the High Street to Wiggenhall Road bordering what was the Wiggenhall Estate, such as the example at the triangle of Wiggenhall Road, Deacon's Hill and Blackwell Drive. From then on the route west follows the Grand Union Canal towards Rickmansworth.

Dealing with the enemy - Prisoners of War

The only way a civilian was likely to meet an enemy soldier was as a prisoner of war. There were 400,000 prisoners of war in Britain between 1939 and 1948. Early in the war the prisoners were usually shot-down Luftwaffe aircrew or captured U-boat crew. It was not until the Allied victories in North Africa that German and Italian ground troops began to arrive in Britain. Although PoWs were held in camps, often buildings converted from other uses, they were given tasks to occupy them. Often these tasks were something useful, for which they were paid union rates, perhaps as construction workers or labourers in the fields, or even employed by the council as dustmen. Some PoWs were put to work over a large area, like Bruno Liebich, based in Batford, who hoed grass, picked potatoes, and laid drainage pipes in winter from Tring to Elstree. Initially prisoners were sent out in working parties, later they could be posted in hostels or housed with a farmer and eventually, like the Italian prisoners set to work in the fields around Borehamwood, became a common sight at work in their distinctive dark clothes with a yellow patch. Some camps were custom built, with Nissen huts, fences, pillboxes and watchtowers. Of the around 600 camps that were eventually put into service, the closest to Watford was Camp 235 near Hemel Hempstead, split between two sites, Gorhambury Park and the 'German Working Camp' at The Arches in Felden – the precise location is unknown. Further afield, in a small camp at Dancer's Hill, South Mimms, near Potters Bar, the prisoners slept in tents (the guards in huts) within a double wire perimeter guarded by two watchtowers. Batford, in Harpenden, conformed to the standard type of camp, as did the Oxhey Lane Camp in Hatch End, just over the border in Middlesex.

At Trent Park near Barnet, a converted mansion enclosed by a double wire perimeter, pillboxes and watchtowers, housed the Combined Services Detailed Interrogation Centre from December 1939 to November 1945. Originally the CSDIC, a branch of MI9 set up for the questioning of selected PoWs by specialist personnel, had its base in the Tower of London, but it was quickly moved to 'Cockfosters Camp', and it was here that captured Luftwaffe aircrews were brought for interrogation. As it was thought aircrew would be more susceptible to giving away information while still in a state of shock after landing, interrogation officers located at RAF stations throughout the country would hurry to the crash site to interview the survivors. It was then decided whether to send them on to Trent Park for further interrogation. In 1942 the organization was expanded to include Latimer House (where Rudolf Hess is said to have been interrogated) and Wilton House in Buckinghamshire. Trent Park was then reserved for high-ranking German generals. The favoured method of eliciting information was by creating a relaxed atmosphere then bugging the inmate's conversations, or by 'planting' an undercover prisoner, usually a Pole in the British services who spoke fluent German, to provoke discussion. The methods revealed intelligence on rocket production, war crimes, and resistance to Hitler.

Spies

A German espionage network already existed within the UK by 1939 and there was a common belief that the country was overrun by professional spies. While propaganda slogans such as 'the walls have ears' and 'careless talk costs lives' reinforced the paranoia, they also reflected a genuine official fear of German fifth columnists and agents. In reality German (and Russian) spies did not come up to the public's imaginings, being ill-trained and poorly motivated. Often speaking with a foreign accent and with poor local knowledge, they would immediately arouse suspicion and were easily rounded up. Many even got cold feet and turned themselves in straight away. One spy, Karel Richard Richter, who had been dropped by parachute near London Colney in May 1941, gave himself away in conversation with a lorry driver. Once arrested he was found to have in his possession a compass, maps, some food and clearly forged identity papers in the name of Fred Snyder that did not match his genuine expired Czechoslovakian passport; he was clearly under-prepared. Richter was executed at Wandsworth prison in December 1942. His mission had been to check up on his fellow agent known as Harry Williamson, real name Wulf Schmidt, who was supposedly living in Barnet.

Wulf Schmidt – double agent

Wulf Schmidt, code name Leonhardt, was a Danish citizen recruited by the *Abwehr*, German military intelligence, because of his ability for languages. He had been parachuted into England in September 1940 with his friend Gösta Caroli in the belief they were preparing for the imminent German invasion. Things went wrong immediately when Caroli was captured near Northampton. Caroli gave their mission away in return for their lives and Schmidt, who had landed in Cambridgeshire, was picked up in Willingham by the Home Guard. The two were sent to Camp 020 at Latchmere House in Richmond where spies were cross-examined by the ace interrogator, the monocle-wearing Lieutenant Colonel Robin Stephens, known as 'Tin-eye'. Schmidt, who expected to be tortured, held out for thirteen days, until his spirit was eventually broken after being offered copious amounts of whiskey. He too had been badly briefed, and on his own admission his desire for self-preservation had meant he was easily turned by MI5 to act as a double agent.

Schmidt, codenamed 'Tate' because of his resemblance to the music-hall comic Harry Tate, became in the view of espionage writer Nigel West, 'one of the seven spies who changed the world'. He became one of MI5's most effective counter-espionage agents in the operation known as the 'Double Cross System' ('XX') which fed the *Abwehr* false intelligence on bomb damage, shipping and troop movements, and factory and air force installations. To test Schmidt's credibility his first task was to use his hidden radio to contact HQ in Hamburg and ask for more funds. In July 1941, in the first of many of XX's complex deceptions known as *Plan Midas* the ante was upped when the Germans were duped into providing £20,000 (variously estimated between £900,000 and £4.8 million today!) via New York to a theatrical agent in London for Schmidt to pick up under the premise that he needed the money to ease information out of officers and officials by passing himself off as a rich black-marketeer at parties thrown by his girlfriend. Schmidt was in reality well away from any London high life, living in quiet seclusion under the assumed name of Harry Williamson with Tommy Robertson, the head of the XX disinformation campaign. MI5 had found premises for their HQ in the prison at Wormwood Scrubs, but Colonel T.A. (Tar) Robertson and his family lived in Round Bush, on the way to Radlett. His wife Joan was also involved with MI5, as a volunteer in the canteen.

Schmidt, sometimes reluctantly, sent over 1,000 false messages. By July 1943 he had been given a new cover story that led the Germans to believe he was required to work on a friend's farm in Radlett to avoid military service; in fact he was working at Greville's Photography in Queen's Road, Watford, and freelancing as a photographer for the *West Herts Post* (his pictures included the V2 bomb damage in Sandringham Road in 1944). As the preparations for D-Day got underway, his fictional farmer friend conveniently got him imaginary work on a farm in Kent so as to observe the troop movements – all part of Operation Bodyguard, the elaborate deception plan to fool the German generals into expecting the allied invasion in the Pas de Calais instead of the Normandy beaches. Schmidt's messages were so successful that ironically his German case officer informed him that his messages 'might even decide the outcome of the war'. With the invasion underway, to retaliate Hitler put his faith in the new technology of the Flying Bomb, but there was a drawback. It was impossible to know its effectiveness without eyes on the ground. Acting as the 'eyes' MI5's double-agents were used to divert the V1 and V2 rockets off target. In February 1945 Churchill was told that messages sent by 'Tate' and a fictional agent 'Rover' had been successfully diverting the missiles, and it is estimated that 11,000 people may have been spared injury or death through misinformation. It was important to try to maintain credibility and some accurate information had to be sent and even birthday wishes to the Führer. His imaginary girlfriend, Mary, worked in American Naval HQ in Grosvenor Square, and at one of her fictitious parties, flush with his 'black market' cash Schmidt supposedly induced a drunken officer to give away the position of newly laid minefields. When the Germans appeared unconvinced with his information Schmidt threatened to quit, demanding why should he take risks if he was only to be ignored. In January 1945 these false minefields were used to divert U-boats from Allied shipping lanes and into more dangerous waters. Schmidt remained in contact with his controllers until 2 May 1945, the day Berlin surrendered to the Russians. In acknowledgement of his contribution to the German war effort 'Tate' had been awarded the Iron Cross first and second-class *in absentia* by radio.

After the war Schmidt, now officially renamed Harry Williamson, was given British citizenship and in 1946 he married Irene Mytton from Letchmore Heath and moved into 55 Leggatts Wood Avenue, North Watford. This may have been yet another cover-up as Harry's MI5 minders had thought he was homosexual. Despite Irene giving birth to a daughter, their relationship did not last; an added strain was that he was still bound by the Official Secrets Act. Whatever the cause, Irene eventually walked out on him taking their daughter. Harry continued as a photographer – in the 1950s his work appeared in the *Watford Observer* and the *Daily Mirror* – while also working as an interpreter and export manager for WEMCO in Wippendell Road until his retirement in 1975. His wartime exploits remained a secret until his cover was finally blown by the publicity surrounding an unpaid poll tax bill. But by 1992, when he died of cancer in hospital aged 80, he had returned to anonymity.

The Hatfield bomb and Agent Zigzag

In 1942 the decoders at Bletchley Park near Milton Keynes intercepted the following cryptic message:

> From Abwehr Nantes to Abwehr HQ Paris, 'Dear France. Your friend Bobby the Pig grows fatter every day. He is gorging now like a king, roars like a lion and shits like an elephant. Fritz'.

They were baffled by the reference to Bobby the Pig, but not by Fritz, they thought they knew who he was: an enemy agent about to be parachuted into England. Bobby was in reality not another agent but the pet pig of the sender of the typically cheeky message, the self-confessed 'honest villain' and safe-blower Eddie Chapman, real name Eddie Wearside, from Newcastle. The elusive Chapman had joined the German secret service as a ruse to get out of Jersey prison where he was serving time when the Channel Islands were occupied in 1940. Under the supervision of Captain Stephan von Gröning of the Nantes *Abwehr* he was trained as a spy and saboteur, and having convinced the Germans of his suitability, he was parachuted into Cambridgeshire in December 1942. His mission was to destroy the de Havilland aircraft factory in Hatfield and cripple the production of Mosquito fighter-bombers. On arrival though, he immediately walked into the nearest police station and declared himself a loyal subject with a desire to work for MI5.

After his interrogation at Latchmere House, MI5 decided to take him on as a double agent, giving him the codename Zigzag. He was put under the supervision of Ronnie Reed, who had controlled Wulf Schmidt (Tate) and his friend Gösta Caroli, (codename Summer). An elaborate double bluff was then planned. Chapman, as agent Zigzag, would carry out his attack on the factory (for which he was paid £15,000). With the aid of Geoffrey de Havilland himself and a number of camouflage experts the correct explosives were chosen to create a realistic explosion and models made that would dupe enemy reconnaissance planes into believing that the factory was destroyed. On the last night of January 1943, a massive nighttime explosion was faked in the power plant, and the inhabitants of Hatfield woke to find a giant 'hole' in the ground and what appeared to be damage everywhere. It was said that Jasper Maskelyne, the famous stage

Eddie Chapman, alias Zigzag, alias Fritz, photographed for MI5 on arrival in England in 1942 (public domain)

illusionist, created the dummy remains, but as it was so soon after the battle of El Alamein in Egypt where he had been working on the fabrication of a ghost army, this assertion has been put into doubt. It is more likely the film set designers from nearby Elstree would have been used. ZigZag reported back to Germany that the plan had been a success and the edition of the *Daily Express* distributed to neutral Portugal ran a short paragraph with photograph saying, 'Investigations are being made into the cause of a factory explosion on the outskirts of London. It is understood that the damage was slight and there was no loss of life.' This report combined with their aerial photographs that seemed to contradict the newspaper convinced the Germans that 'Fritz' had done a good job. In MI5's own words, 'one of the most remarkable deception operations of the Second World War' had been carried out.

Chapman's MI5 handlers decided that the next step was to persuade the Germans that he should return to Germany, a move that could be of great advantage. Reluctantly the Germans agreed. After pretending to plant bombs on board *The City of Lancaster*, the ship that had taken him from Liverpool to Lisbon, supposedly to destroy it on its return journey (they were 'discovered' just in time), he was able to convince any sceptics in the *Abwehr* of his loyalty. Chapman's charm worked so well on the Germans, particularly on von Gröning, that 'Fritz' was endearingly turned into Fritchen, taken into the German army as an *oberleutnant* (first lieutenant) and awarded the Iron Cross. In addition, he was handsomely rewarded financially (while still being paid by MI5), even receiving his own yacht. In Oslo, where he was sent to train German spies, he had an affair with Dagmar Lahlum of the Norwegian Resistance. She did not realize at first that he was a British agent, but once she was aware of the situation, they worked together gathering information on the German command. After the war, Dagmar's perceived collaboration meant that she served six months in prison for consorting with a German officer, unable to prove her innocence because she thought Chapman was dead.

In 1944 von Gröning decided to send Chapman back to England to help direct the V1 rockets to their targets. In the same way as Schmidt, his information guided the rockets so that they either overshot or undershot their target, London. Some may have landed harmlessly in fields, but there was the calculated risk that some would inevitably hit built-up areas, such as the ones that caused damage in Watford.

Chapman's handlers were unconvinced of his ability to lead an honest life, and after the war, true to form he fell back in with the criminal fraternity. By 1953 his ill-gotten gains enabled him to buy the thirty-two room Shenley Lodge where he opened a health resort with his wife, Betty Farmer, who had been his pre-war girlfriend. Still on good terms with Stephan von Gröning, he invited his former German spy boss to his daughter Suzanne's wedding. Chapman's wartime exploits were made into a film, *Triple Cross* (1967), with Christopher Plummer as Chapman, which proved another good little earner. Ever the tale-spinner, he was reputed to have kept the locals in the Black Lion in Shenley entertained with his yarns until his death in 1997.

Secret Missions, intelligence gathering and the SOE

A number of large Hertfordshire houses within easy reach of London were quickly requisitioned, and some proved ideal bases for secret operations. The target of the *Abwehr*'s agent Fritz had been the de Havilland factory where the Mosquito was manufactured. Despite Fritz's apparent success, by 1943 the Mosquito had become one of the war's most successful aircraft, so much so that Hermann Göring, the commander-in-chief of the *Luftwaffe*, was furious with jealousy. It irked him that the British, who had easy access to aluminium, would chose to have every piano factory knocking together at an ever increasing speed 'a beautiful wooden aircraft' because 'they have the geniuses and we have the nincompoops'. One of these geniuses was the aviation pioneer Geoffrey de Havilland. Realising that there was no room for slack capacity in the modern form of 'total war' where all enterprise had to be geared to the war effort, de Havilland saw an opportunity to utilize the resources and skills of the furniture industry. In 1939 the de Havilland

Company took over Salisbury Hall, in London Colney, near to their factory in Hatfield. The former residence of Nell Gwynne and Lady Randolph Churchill (mother of Winston) was then put to use for the secret development of their prototype fighter-bomber. Nicknamed 'the wooden wonder' and made from a mixture of ply, spruce and balsa wood, it may have sounded like a glorified model aircraft, but with its two Rolls Royce Merlin engines it was fast and manoeuvrable, outperforming the Spitfire and capable of carrying the same payload as a B-17 Flying Fortress to Berlin (albeit in one 4,000lb bomb or four 500lb bombs); plus, its greatest asset, its extreme versatility. Although when operating solely as a bomber it was unarmed, the small crew and speed of the plane meant that it proved safer to fly in than the Lancaster or the B-17.

As was often the case with innovation in Britain, de Havilland began the development of their revolutionary design in 1938 in the face of official scepticism and lack of support. The company moved their design team from Hatfield to Salisbury Hall, using the barn at the back of the house as a secret hangar, and it was here that the first Mosquito was made. After numerous interruptions and delays incurred by other priorities (the Battle of Britain, Dunkirk), eventually the chief obstacle, Lord Beaverbrook, who was Minister of Aircraft production, was finally convinced. After visits from Winston Churchill and various Air Ministry officials, the prototype was dismantled and taken by lorry to de Havilland's airstrip at Hatfield where it began test flights during November 1940; but it was not until September 1941 that the Mosquito became fully operational.

Late in 1940, the secluded recesses of Bucknalls, a large Victorian house on the fringe of Watford towards Leavesden surrounded by thirty-eight acres of land, became important in the development of one of the most famous exploits of the war. The house is the headquarters of the Building Research Establishment who have occupied the site since 1925 after moving there from Acton. War required the staff to be deployed in different kinds of work and in early 1941 three trusted members were put to secretly creating a 1:50 scale model of the Mohne dam on the river Ruhr across a brook in a wooded part of the grounds. Made out of two million scaled-down mortar blocks around a concrete core, it took them seven weeks to build. Once completed, the model was to be used to test the effectiveness of a bouncing bomb. The bomb, codename 'Upkeep', was the brainchild of Barnes Wallis, an engineer employed by Vickers who had previously invented a geodetic airframe system used in fuselage and wing manufacture for Wellington bombers. The tests were needed to determine where a bomb should hit the dam for maximum effect, how heavy it should be and with how much explosive, before attempting full-scale trials. In December 1940, Wallis had secretly met with Dr Norman Davey, designer of the Royal Albert Hall's acoustic dome and Head of Engineering at BRE, and outlined to him how the bomb was to be used. Davey then set in motion the making of a tiny replica dam, followed by the building of the 3ft high by 42ft long version on which small explosives were used. The trials took some time and it was not until May 1942 that explosive bouncing bombs were used on the disused Nant-y-Gro dam in Wales, followed by tests in January 1943 to assess the suitability of Lancaster bombers at Chesil Beach. Operation Chastise, more famously known as the Dam Busters Raid, then took place on the night of 16 May when nineteen bombers of 617 Squadron (Squadron X) under Wing Commander Guy Gibson attacked the Mohne and Sorpe dams on the Ruhr and the Edersee dam on the Eder. The Mohne and Edersee were breached, flooding the Ruhr and Eder valleys and causing significant damage to industry and loss of life. Davey showed the model, which still exists, to the makers of the film *The Dam Busters* in 1955, too late to be included. Norman Davey is locally also remembered for his involvement in the 1931/2 excavation of Roman Verulamium with Sir Mortimer Wheeler and the restorations of the wall paintings and mosaics in St Albans museum.

The isolated and secluded Barnes Lodge in Kings Langley, sadly demolished in 1976, was requisitioned as a long-range listening and receiving station early in the war. Unknown to most of the locals, 127 people were employed there in 'war work'. One of a chain of 95 stations spread across Europe, it was linked by cable to transmitters in Chipperfield House and to Tower Hill where there were 46 radio towers, and by landline to the 6th Bureau of the Polish General Staff in London SW1. The Polish government in exile maintained links with the homeland through Radio Polski, broadcast on BBC wavelengths, and in August 1944 the BBC Monitory Service picked up return broadcasts from radio station 'Błyskawica' (lightning) run by the Polish underground. This was to be particularly significant as in anticipation of the Red Army's advance on Warsaw the Polish Home Army, the major resistance movement allied to the government in exile, organized a revolt in the capital to force the Germans out. At Barnes Lodge, Polish telegraphists picked up the broadcasts from Poland that gave important information on the progress of what became known as the 'Warsaw Uprising' and the German reprisals, recording them on disc.

The events of the summer of 1944 became highly controversial and in retrospect are seen as the opening rounds of the Cold War. Having initially promised assistance, Stalin held the Red Army back, claiming the Poles had acted too soon, and blocked British and American assistance to the Polish fighters until it was too late. By October, the resistance was defeated and Warsaw razed to the ground by the Germans. Around 16,000 resistance fighters were killed, but the death toll of the aftermath was even worse when 200,000 civilians lost their lives, many in mass executions. Although many felt that Stalin had allowed the uprising to fail for his own ends, for propaganda purposes it was thought best to keep alive the myth of a unified alliance between Britain, the USA and the Soviet Union. The details of the failure were glossed over, some of the records of the event disappeared, and it is thought likely that the discs kept at Barnes Lodge were censored. In effect, the new era of distrust between the West and Russia had begun as Stalin began to carve out his sphere of interest in Eastern Europe.

There were other Poles in the area working on high-level intelligence work. In 1943, Henryk Zygalski took a rented room at the home of Bertha Blofield in Bury Rise, Bovingdon. He had spent three years dodging the German advance before arriving in the relative peace of rural Hertfordshire. A mathematician before the war he had become a cryptologist in Poland in the late 1930s and had designed a system of perforated sheets for decoding the German Enigma messages. The information gleaned by the Poles was then passed on to the British and French forces and a Polish mock-up of the Enigma machine found its way to Bletchley Park where it would contribute to its eventual decoding. When Poland fell, Zygalski fled with his Polish colleagues to France where they spent much of their time on the run. After stays in Toulouse and Paris and even North Africa, they were forced to flee once again after the fall of France. Zygalski eventually escaped via Spain and Portugal to England, where he and his colleague Jerzy Rózycki were assigned to the Communication Unit of the Polish Supreme Command based at Boxmoor. Zygalski worked on breaking SS codes at the Shendish Dower House in Kings Langley. After the war, Poland under the Communist regime was not welcoming to returning exiles, and like many of his compatriots he remained in England, slipping into a life of anonymity as a lecturer in mathematics, his work as a cryptologist remaining unknown for many years under the Official Secrets Act.

The top secret Special Operations Executive (SOE) was formed in 1940 with the purpose of carrying out espionage, sabotage and reconnaissance and supporting resistance movements in occupied Europe and later south-east Asia. Known by a select few as 'The Baker Street Irregulars', 'Churchill's Secret Army', or the 'Ministry of Ungentlemanly Warfare', to the outside world its activities were hidden discretely behind the mundane sounding 'Joint Technical Board' or the 'Inter Service Research Bureau'. The organisation employed 13,000 men and women in over 70 requisitioned establishments. Referred to ironically as the 'Stately 'omes of England', these included garages, cottages and even some large country mansions. In the style of 'Q', the head of the fictional research and development branch of the secret service in the James Bond movies, SOE specialised in the invention of an array of mysterious gadgets for their agents. Ian Fleming, Bond's creator, worked in Naval intelligence and would have seen the inventions demonstrated in the rooms of SOE's station in the Natural History Museum's Tring premises. His inspiration for Q was Charles Fraser-Smith, who commuted from his home in Croxley Green with his neighbour, the scientist Sir Bernard Spilsbury, to his London office near St James's Park, neither realising they were both working on the same secret project, Operation Mincemeat. This was a plot hatched by Fleming to supply false information to the Germans about the D-Day landings using a corpse (the 'Man Who Never Was') washed up on the Spanish coast.

SOE had thirty-three Special Training Schools in Hertfordshire and around 1942 Fleming was working at the training school at Roughwood Park near Chorleywood. The first STS establishment was at Brickendonbury Manor at Brickendon. Shenley Lodge, the future home of agent ZigZag (Eddie Chapman), was another. The running of the schools was heavily reliant on the assistance of the women of the First Aid Nursing Yeomanry. Despite the name of their organisation, over half the women of FANY were involved in running the schools as auxiliaries and some directly in carrying out espionage. The name was not a complete misnomer – the women of FANY did receive training in first aid – but they could also drive trucks and ambulances, handle small arms and explosives, and use wireless and ciphers.

Kim Philby, who later became infamous as 'the Third Man', one of the five Cambridge spies passing secrets to the Russians during the Cold War, was instrumental in setting up the Brickendonbury Manor School. Already a KGB agent when he was recruited by MI6, he became a member of Section V working on counter-intelligence where he became one of the few people allowed to see the ULTRA transcripts from Bletchley Park. SOE had taken two houses next to one another in St Albans; Prae Wood House, where the Central Registry was housed, and Glenalmond (Station XB), a large Edwardian house in King Harry Lane. Once posted to Glenalmond, Philby could get access to the registry files of agents working in the field, including those in Russia. The sudden influx of young people staying at Glenalmond might have aroused interest from the locals. The occupants, who could be found frequently propping up the bar in the King Harry public house, posed as archaeologists working on the ruins of Verulamium to quell any curiosity. Philby, who had been put in charge of the operation to counter German espionage activities in neutral Spain and Portugal, was also required to teach the art of black propaganda to the agents under his supervision, including Malcolm Muggeridge, Graham Greene, Ivan Ustinov (father of the actor Peter) and fellow Soviet spy John Cairncross. All the while he was faithfully passing on information to Moscow.

Philby's spymasters nearly put paid to his activities as a double agent when they decided to test his reliability by asking for the identities of British agents working in the Soviet Union. Captain William Woodfield, the chief registrar at Prae House, was a regular drinker at the King Harry and it proved an easy task for Philby to obtain the relevant files by replenishing his glass with numerous pink gins. Unfortunately for Philby the files showed there was no British spy network in Russia at that time; the war with Germany was of greater priority, information that only aroused more suspicion back in Moscow. Of more immediate concern, Captain Woodfield suddenly requested the files to be returned, files that contained material well outside his brief, but they could not be found. On the brink of the matter being reported to 'C', Sir Stewart Menzies, the head of MI6, it transpired that Woodfield's secretary, who had been off with a bout of flu, had combined them with other volumes to save shelf space. If she been off for longer, or if Woodfield had been more sober, Philby's career as a master spy would have been swiftly terminated. Instead he continued to successfully deceive MI6 (sending 100 agents to their deaths in communist Albania in 1945) while being awarded the OBE and touted as a future head of the department. Philby had a number of close calls, almost being convicted of treason in 1952 and 1955, before he was finally exposed in 1963. During their time at Glenalmond, Philby and Greene became friends, and Greene remained loyal to Philby after he defected, visiting him five times in Moscow. Before D-Day Glenalmond was turned over to the French to train their agents in intelligence gathering.

The technical side of putting agents into the field was well represented in South West Hertfordshire with a number of SOE experimental stations. The activities at these sites ranged from storage and production, training, research and development, to administration. At Station VI, Bride Hall near Ayot St Lawrence, the task was weapons acquisition. Station IX, The Frythe estate near Welwyn Garden City, was involved in wireless research (Special Signals), then weapons development and production, and then research and development; today it is a factory belonging to GlaxoSmithKline. Station XI, Old Gorhambury House near St Albans, was for accommodation. At Station XII, Aston House near Stevenage, alongside production, packaging and dispatch, 'boffins' in the laboratory produced an array of items in which the agents could conceal codes and messages; and at Station XVII, Brickendonbury Manor, where the limpet mine was invented by Stuart Macrae, explosive trials were carried out and training in industrial sabotage. Important successes from the work at Brickendonbury were Operation Frankton, the commando attack by canoe on shipping in Bordeaux harbour in 1942 commonly known as the 'Cockleshell Heroes' raid, the destruction in 1943 of the Norsk Hydro heavy water plant in Telemark, Norway, and the bombing of the Renault factory in France to disrupt Germany's nuclear bomb programme. Josef Gabčík and Jan Kubiš trained at Brickendonbury before their mission to assassinate Heydrich, *Reichsprotektor* of Bohemia and Moravia (Operation Anthropoid) in May 1942. Today it is the more peaceful Research Laboratory for the Malaysian Rubber Research Development Board.

Ken Ward, a captain in the Royal Signals, worked for ISRB (Interservices Research Bureau), Radiocommunications Division (RCD), cover-name for the ultra-secret Radio Research Development and Manufacture of Communications Equipment. When he was posted to The Frythe (Station IX) in January 1942 he described it as a 'Queer spot! What have I got into? Blue Cap security police, miscellaneous soldiers, airmen, sailors and civilians, all in a stately pile with sundry wooden huts in the grounds.' The brief for his division's work there was to design, manufacture and provide all communication needs for the SOE personnel operating in the field. What he discovered in the laboratory was around forty-two projects on the go at one time and it was from there a number of ingenious bits of equipment were dreamt up: a fold-up motorbike to be dropped by parachute (the Welbike), a one-man submarine (the Welman), a motorized submersible canoe and various concealable firearms – the sort of stuff that would eventually find their way into James Bond's fantasy arsenal.

The RCD section was known as Station VII and split into Manufacture (VIIA), Supplies and Liaison with Industry (VIIB), The Laboratory (VIIC), and later Airborne Equipment (VIID). Captain Ward's responsibilities as Contract Liaison were to 'find and arrange supply of the necessary components, materials and equipment required, ensuring the ability of contractors and factory staff to deliver top quality work on time, ensuring availability of parts etc at all times to meet lab needs.' This involved close contact with numerous local firms, and the constant search for larger premises and factory capacity. VIIB was eventually moved to the Yeast-Vite factory in Watford. Yeast-Vite, makers of foodstuffs in Whippendell Road where the famous pills were produced, became the base for goods receiving, inspection and test, stores, packing and dispatch. There was 'special out storage for valves etc' in Kidderminster, because 'the valves did not react favourably to nearby bomb blasts.' A month or two later VIIC (the Laboratory) was moved close to VIIB in Allensor's Joinery Works, whose premises were in King Gregory Avenue off Wippendell Road. Like Yeast-Vite, they had no previous experience of wireless. The field and base stations equipment and other special needs had to be scrounged from whatever source and the assemblage of transmitters, masts, rigging and cables gathered into 'suitcases' that might be whisked off to a group fighting in Yugoslavia at any moment.

Station XV, the Camouflage Section of SOE was based at The Thatched Barn, a former out-of-town entertainment venue situated on the corner of the Barnet bypass. The building had been bought for redevelopment in a moment of bad timing by Billy Butlin, founder of the holiday camps, just before the outbreak of the war. Close to the Elstree film studios in Borehamwood and with easy access to London, it had been a glamorous stopping off point, boasting Bette Davis and other film stars as visitors throughout the '30s. At the beginning of the war, Elstree Studios closed and were turned over to use as an ordnance depot and a garrison theatre for the army. In consequence, the Barn, once considered the height of luxury with its elaborate dining hall and heated outdoor swimming pool, became the incongruous setting under the SOE for former studio workers to use their skills to create exploding props such as bicycle pumps, cigarettes or stuffed rats under the supervision of Colonel J. Elder Willis, an RAF veteran of the First World War and experienced art director in civilian life. In the strictest secrecy, agents on their way to France might be equipped there with reproduction French clothing (copied from newspaper photographs and catalogues and perfect down to the last detail) or maps hand sewn into silk underwear. They might also be given elaborate or outrageous disguises, even to the extent of false humpbacks. The specifications of the exploding bicycle pump read: 'A hollow brass cylinder filled with explosive and fitted with a pull switch, is pushed inside the barrel of a bicycle pump [and] the safety pin withdrawn. The enemy's pump is replaced by the explosive one and his tyres deflated.' Ways of concealing weapons were devised: hand grenades packed into fruit tins with labels skillfully reproduced by artists to look like the real thing, or Sten guns inside painted Plaster of Paris 'wooden' logs. After the war the Thatched Barn featured as a location in a number of film and television productions for Elstree Studios including *The Saint* with Roger Moore and *The Prisoner* with Patrick McGoohan. The building lay derelict for a number of years until it was demolished in the late 1980s. More prosaically, and hopefully calmly for the guests, the site is occupied by the Holiday Inn today.

One of the SOE agents that the 'boffins' of Hertfordshire would have equipped was Francis Cammaerts. Francis was the son of Émile Cammaerts, a Belgian playwright, poet (who had written war poetry in the First World War) and professor at the University of London who lived in Hillside road, Radlett. Like many of his generation, Francis became a pacifist while at Cambridge University and he tried to register as a conscientious objector. After an appeal his local tribunal granted his request on condition that he took up agricultural work, and he was posted to the Lincolnshire Peace Community farm at Holden Hall. His attitude changed, however, on the death of his brother Pieter, a pilot in the RAF (buried in Radlett Church). He now felt he could no longer stand aside, and on the urging of his friend Harry Rée, also a former conscientious objector, in 1942 he joined him in the SOE where he could use his knowledge of French. Despite the disadvantage for undercover work of being conspicuously tall at 6ft 3ins, from 1943 onwards he served successfully in occupied France with the resistance, organizing sabotage (particularly after D-Day) and getting arrested and then freed by the Gestapo. His efforts earned him promotion to lieutenant colonel, the DSO, the Légion d'Honneur, the Croix de Guerre and the American Medal of Freedom. Francis's sister Catherine was the mother of the author Michael Morpurgo, the writer of the acclaimed children's book *Warhorse.* After the war Francis went back into teaching like his friend Harry Rée DSO, who became headmaster of Watford Boys Grammar School in 1951.

General de Gaulle in Berkhamsted

When German forces were flooding into France in May 1940, Charles de Gaulle was in command of the French 4th Armoured Division. In recognition of his attempts to hold back the German advance he was promoted to brigadier general, a title he retained for the rest of his life, and given the post of Under-Secretary for National Defence and War in the government. Once France capitulated, and it became apparent that Pétain's government would collaborate with Hitler, de Gaulle decided to come to London from where he could organize his Free French forces and form a government in exile in opposition to the official army and newly-formed Vichy government in France. From London he began to make radio broadcasts to rally French resistance to the Nazi occupation. At first, his broadcasts went largely unnoticed but eventually they would gather an audience of millions, making him a traitor in the eyes of the Vichy government who condemned him to death.

Like the statues from London's parks and buildings that were hidden in the grounds of Berkhamsted Castle in 1941, de Gaulle found himself and his family transported by the British government away from the London blitz to the relative safety of Rodinghead House, home of a Colonel Johns, in Little Gaddesden next to the Ashridge Estate. There was still danger from the odd bomb, like those that destroyed the railway bridge in Berkhamsted, and de Gaulle converted the cellar of the house into an air raid shelter. To boost French morale and aid the Free French cause, Winston Churchill instigated propaganda pictures to be taken showing the family relaxing in their pleasant villa surroundings. Rodinghead was close enough to London for de Gaulle to continue his radio broadcasts and keep contact with his fellow officers, such as Colonel Passy, the Free French head of intelligence, who was a regular visitor.

As a potential assassination target de Gaulle's presence was kept quiet, and his bodyguards were probably never far away. Even so, as a practising Catholic, he and his family could be spotted attending mass regularly at the Church of the Sacred Heart at Park View Road in Berkhamsted (after the war a nursery school) and on Remembrance Sunday in 1941 he was photographed taking the salute with the Home Guard at Potten End. His relations with Winston Churchill (with whom he constantly argued), the SOE and his hosts were often strained and, forever the staunch patriot, he was apparently furious that day because no one could find a French flag. Often thought to be prickly and arrogant, de Gaulle resented being treated as subordinate by his allies. Although he was able to make a triumphal return to liberated Paris on 25 August 1944, at the head of his own 4th Armoured Division and the Free French, he had to do so accompanied by the US army. Until then he had been dependent on Churchill's support and British help in organizing French resistance. In the end his time in exile was the making of his political career as leader of the French government and the future President of France.

CHAPTER FOUR

The War in the Air

Warfare had taken to the air during the Great War and the civilian population subjected to aerial bombardment for the first time. Terrifying as this had been, it was merely a hint of what was to come. The great technological advances achieved since, especially in aviation, meant that warfare would be carried out on an unprecedented scale. Air power was to be a significant factor in the prosecution of the war effort for both sides. The manufacture of fighters, initially to defend British skies, and of bombers, to take the war to the enemy, required workers, and the location of airfields and the sight of enemy bombers in the sky brought the war close to home. As before, Watford's proximity to London put it on the front line, but the area was also important in its own right as a base for taking the fight back to the enemy.

The Battle of Britain

In the summer of 1940, Hitler attempted to bring Britain to its knees before launching an invading force by achieving aerial superiority. To achieve this the Luftwaffe needed to knock out the RAF by targeting its airfields, supporting industry, ports and infrastructure. But Hitler soon became impatient with their lack of success and switched the brunt of the attack to the cities and the civilian population with London taking most of the punishment in a series of devastating night attacks known as the Blitz. For nearly a year (July 1940 to May 1941) the British people experienced war as never before. No one was immune. To get fighters into the air in time to engage with the enemy and to warn the people of an impending raid, a system of defence was put in place known as the Dowding System. When the sirens sounded, it meant that the bombers had breached the first line in the defences provided by the RAF. Then it was time for those on the ground to dash for the shelters while the anti-aircraft gunners would open fire.

RAF Coastal Command was based at Northwood in the grounds of Eastbury Park, and London and southern England were defended by Group 11 Fighter Command from a number of airfields across the region run from Hillingdon House. The closest airfields to the Watford area were Stapleford Tawney in Essex and Hendon, Northolt and Uxbridge. The response was coordinated from the headquarters of Fighter Command at Bentley Priory. A grand eighteenth-century house, with additions by the architect Sir John

Soane, built on the site of a cell of Augustinian Friars, Bentley Priory had been the former residence of the Marquess of Abercorn, Queen Adelaide, the aunt of Queen Victoria, a hotel and a girls' school. The Air Ministry bought it as an empty building in 1926, provided an airstrip for visiting dignitaries and installed the Inland Area (Training Command), part of the Air Defence of Great Britain (ADGB), until the creation of Fighter Command in 1936 under Air Chief Marshal Sir Hugh Dowding. During the Battle of Britain, Bentley Priory would play a vital role in coordinating the air defences against enemy bombers. As the hub for the Royal Observer Corps, relocated there from RAF Uxbridge, approaching enemy aircraft were tracked from there as they crossed the coastline so that notice could be given for air-raid warnings and to intercepting fighters. Group 11 and the Balloon Centre at RAF Stanmore Park were directly under the control of Bentley Priory. For protection against bombing the site was camouflaged and there were dugouts and cellars. Despite being such an important target it sustained only slight damage from two small bombs and a V2 rocket.

Around 150 officers and airmen and 84 civilians were employed on the site and Bushey Heath became a residential area for RAF personnel. In 1940 the RAF commandeered Hartsbourne Manor, formerly the home of the American actress and socialite Maxine Elliott, to house the officers. A great favourite of King Edward VII, she was famous for hosting lavish parties for her fiancé, the New Zealand tennis ace Captain Tony Wilding (who died in 1915), and guests that included Winston Churchill, F.E. Smith (later Lord Birkenhead), and the financier Pierpont Morgan. The subsequent occupiers, the Wembley Golf Club, had only had the building for a short while, having been required to move there in 1928 to make way for the new twin-towered Wembley football stadium. The house resumed its former golfing use when the Hartsbourne Country Club took it over after the war. The houses nearby were also occupied, notably those in Prowse Avenue by Air Vice Marshal Alfred Iredell CB, the Chief Medical Officer, and Air Vice Marshal Harry George CBE, CO of No 17 (Operational Training) Group, Coastal Command. George was a first world war DFC and he went on to distinguish himself in Iraq in 1941. Amongst the other residences in Bushey Heath were seven timber kit or ranch-style houses in Elstree Road built during the '20s and '30s and given as a gift by the Canadian government to the RAF in recognition of their assistance in the First World War. The kit-houses were exported by the British Columbia Building Company and housed officers from the Priory. Rosary Priory, the convent school in Caldecote Towers, acted as a hostel for the Bentley Priory WAAFs.

When the fortunes of war were reversed the Priory became a planning centre for the D-Day landings where events were monitored by King George V, Winston Churchill and Eisenhower in the Allied Expeditionary Force war room. Much of the more detailed work was carried out nearby in Kestrel

Grove in Hive Road, Bushey Heath. Here the 'plotters', the young WAAFs that are a feature of every war movie planning sequence, would move little tin arrows over a large table-top map. Some of the young women involved in this around-the-clock top-secret work came from as far afield as Northern Ireland. Rosemary Morgan who served in the WAAF at Kestrel Grove recalled her impression of the D-Day War Room:

> When we arrived in this dark room we were in front of a large table map of the English Channel and everyone was agog, not knowing if this was an exercise or the real thing! No one wanted to leave. In the morning we were taken up to another room which was entered by a series of curtains so that nothing inside could be seen from the corridor. This large room was brightly lit with a large table in the centre and on the wall opposite was a large map of Britain and most of Europe.

The Allied military 'top brass', including a liaison officer from the Free French, would begin their conference at 11 am, during which time 'All the staff had to go to a small room out of hearing so that security was complete.' Then there was a division of labour between army and air force; as the ATS shadowed the progress of the army across France on the map with little red lines, the WAAF pinned little cardboard 'bombs' to places that had been hit the previous day. Afterwards both would hoover the carpet as the cleaning ladies were not allowed in. Kestrel Grove ceased its military use with the end of the war in Europe (today it is a retirement home), but Bentley Priory continued to be used by the RAF until 2008, after which it was turned into a residential development, retaining the old officers' mess as a museum.

In June 1940 the Aldenham Lodge Hotel in Radlett was requisitioned as the headquarters of the newly formed and secret RAF Radio Counter-Measures (RCM) unit, whose purpose was to create electronic counter-measures (ECM) for jamming German radio navigation systems and intelligence on enemy radio and radar. In its heyday the Lodge may have boasted a restaurant, a cocktail lounge, TV and billiards, but it was remembered by its new occupants for its investment by cockroaches and rats. The swimming pool at least was regularly used by some of the 21 officers and 200 other ranks. Married men were housed in Radlett. The unit was renamed No. 80 (Signals) Wing in October, with the motto 'Confusion to Our Enemies'. A year later its operations room moved to larger premises nearby at 'Newberries', probably part of the Porters Golf Club where anti-tank traps and a pillbox still can be seen. By 1942 it had a flying wing and in 1943 it was transferred again to Handley Page's Radlett airfield as part of 100 (Bomber Support) Group where they developed specialist equipment to be fitted to de Havilland Mosquitoes.

There were no operational airfields close to Watford in the early stages. It was not until the end of 1941 when the balance of the war began to shift that the RAF could go on the offensive and it was then that RAF Bovingdon came into existence. A standard RAF bomber airfield, it had a main NE/SW runway 1,634 yards long and two secondary runways of 1,433 yards. This meant it was never developed into a full heavy-bomber airfield as it did not have the required 2,000 yards runway. No. 7 Group Bomber Command took up residence in June 1942 and began flying operational missions, but the airfield would become more famous when it was taken over by the USAAF Eighth Air Force that August.

As the war progressed, the expansion of the RAF and then the Allied response meant there became a greater need for more airfield facilities and infrastructure. The technical training of RAF personnel had been a makeshift affair until RAF Mill Green, near Hatfield, was opened in 1942 to replace the efforts of a local private firm, Jack Olding and Co, the main dealer in Caterpillar earth moving equipment and Deere tractors, who had provided their services at no cost to the taxpayer. Mill Green housed the No. 2 School of Airfield Construction, part of the RAF No. 24 Group Technical Training Command, and, by 1943, the 5351 Airfield Construction Workshop used for training in plant maintenance and repair.

CHAPTER FIVE

On the Defensive

This morning the British Ambassador in Berlin handed the German Government a final note stating that, unless we heard from them by 11 o'clock that they were prepared at once to withdraw their troops from Poland, a state of war would exist between us. I have to tell you now that no such undertaking has been received, and that consequently this country is at war with Germany.

Neville Chamberlain's BBC broadcast, 11 am, 3 September 1939

Creating the Home Front

The memory of Chamberlain's Sunday morning broadcast announcing that the country was in 'a state of war' would become etched in the nation's collective memory. He went on to say that he expected everyone to play their part in the ensuing conflict for which the government had prepared, whether

> *... in the fighting services or as a volunteer in one of the branches of Civil Defence. If so you will report for duty in accordance with the instructions you have received. You may be engaged in work essential to the prosecution of war for the maintenance of the life of the people - in factories, in transport, in public utility concerns, or in the supply of other necessaries of life. If so, it is of vital importance that you should carry on with your jobs.*

It was a moment for which most of the population had resigned itself, but unfortunately not all were psychologically prepared. When, to emphasise the veracity of the PM's words, the air raid sirens were sounded, the wail apparently had the undesired effect of causing the area's first fatality, Mrs Ethel Potter of the White Hart, Bushey, who died of shock. Caught up in the excitement some ARP wardens rashly took to ringing alarm bells, the warning for an imminent gas attack, with the result that window-shoppers in the High Street were hastily fumbling for their gas masks.

The fact that Sunday strollers were already carrying gas masks underlines the level of anticipation. Thirty-eight million masks had already been given out door to door to families, including for young children and babies; now came the more serious business of trying them out in earnest.

WILLS'S CIGARETTES

THE CIVILIAN RESPIRATOR—
HOW TO REMOVE IT

WILLS'S CIGARETTES

THE CIVILIAN RESPIRATOR

Advice on how to wear a gas mask from Wills cigarette cards (Bushey Museum)

The *Watford Observer* informed its readers that air-raid siren practices would take place at lunchtime on the first Sunday of every month. The danger of air attack meant that landmarks that could be seen from the air had to be disguised. In consequence two large pipes that dominated the skyline above the reservoir supplying Watford in Attenborough Fields, Bushey, were removed; and these precautions combined with anti-German feeling prompted the demolition of Lululand, the former residence of the artist Hubert von Herkomer. The minor inconvenience of the removal of place names and changing of signposts in an effort to confuse enemy paratroopers had begun the previous Tuesday, implying that the threat of imminent air-borne invasion was real enough. The implementation of the 'blackout' followed on the Friday and was succeeded by an array of small measures that accumulatively would dominate the daily round for the next five years. Public transport services were cut back to save fuel, and parts of the system put to military use. Two days before the declaration of war, 400 London Green Line buses had already been taken out of service and converted into ambulances in the short space of five hours. The following Friday (8 September) ration books appeared, available on application at local taxation or post offices, in preparation for the petrol rationing that came into force the following week. The same day it became apparent that ordinary pleasures could no longer be taken for granted when the Football Association suspended the new football season after only three matches 'until official notice to the contrary'.

Even though the front line might be on foreign soil or at sea, advances in airpower meant the enemy's greater reach would blur the distinction between

Sign being painted out at Bushey and Oxhey station. The men were instructed to paint out the name, but they left the ampersand and the station was henceforth known as Ampersand Station. Unfortunately the lettering can still be read anyway. The ruling lasted until autumn 1942 (Bushey Museum)

civilian and combatant. Aerial bombardment and the real threat of invasion meant civilians were under direct threat as never before, and precautions had to be put into immediate effect. The resources needed to keep the nation on a war footing would be such that virtually no corner of life could escape being turned to the 'war effort'. This gave the term 'Home Front' even more significance, as those living and working behind the lines felt they too were contributing alongside the military. Straight away the signs of militarization became apparent as volunteers, including the nurses, were set to filling sandbags to protect the Peace Memorial Hospital. Hospitals, schools and other public buildings and spaces were soon made almost invisible behind their walls of sandbags, and rail stations needed extra signs to indicate the location of the entrance for passengers. In addition it was necessary to get used to windows being covered with tape to counter the shattering of glass during a bomb blast.

The older generation may have despaired but local school children were thrilled to know that the declaration of war gave them an extra two weeks holiday. Schools opened on 21 September after adequate air raid precautions and safety measures had been installed. Perhaps for those lucky enough to enjoy it, for the rest of the war schooling would be disrupted from the norm,

Civil Defence volunteers, some in decontamination kit, engaged in an exercise using a derelict house. The same photo appeared in the West Herts Post, *November 1939 (Bushey Museum)*

often by frequent air raid warnings, and school buildings turned over to other uses. When term resumed it was a haphazard affair. Classes might be held in shifts, or, as in the case of Watford Boys Grammar School, on alternate days. Children were required to take their uncomfortable gas masks to school, where the effectiveness of the masks would be tested. To overcome their reluctance to putting on the masks they would be worn for short periods in class. Adults had to be trained in their use too. Shoppers were subjected to a simulated gas attack on Watford High Street. Strategically placed canisters of tear gas were set off and the shopping area became filled with fumes. People put on their masks and took shelter in shops until the gas dispersed. Over time, as the threat of a gas attack subsided, people became careless and increasingly left their gas masks at home.

At night windows were hidden by heavy curtains, with the addition of cardboard or paint if necessary to prevent the leakage of any light, in compliance with the blackout enforced by the patrolling ARP wardens. This

Bushey Civil Defence ambulance ladies with their Packard converted bakery van ambulance and in decontamination gear with their dog (also wearing an 'A' for ambulance helmet) with ARP van behind, c.1940/41 (Bushey Museum)

was done in town and country alike, a reminder that the danger of aerial attack was not to be confined to urban areas. Cawdells department store in the High Street was on hand to supply all your blackout needs and the purchase of Anderson shelters was advertised in the local press. Street-lamps were switched off and car and bus headlamps partially covered, leaving three hooded slits allowing a small beam of light through. Unsurprisingly there was an increase in the number of accidents, so as a safety measure curbs in the road and the bumpers of vehicles were painted white. It was the duty of the wardens to pounce on every blackout lapse, however trivial. In the first week a miscreant was fined £1 for allowing light from his cellar to be visible and six youths were fined for lighting cigarettes during an alert. Such severe enforcements of the rules often made the wardens the butt of people's resentment at the restrictions imposed on their new life. In time the populace would learn the hard way the necessity for vigilance. The maligned wardens oversaw more than the imposition of the blackout. As members of the Air Raid Precautions, which numbered around one and a half million personnel, mostly volunteers, they helped to put up air raid shelters and provided first-on-the-scene medical assistance. The ARP, renamed Civil Defence in 1941, included rescue and stretcher (or first-aid) parties, control centre staff and messenger boys, and their work often overlapped with the fire and medical services and the WVS.

The responsibility for civil defence fell on local authorities and the provision of shelters was a major problem. Watford Council set up an Air Raid Shelters Sub-Committee that considered various proposals through 1939 into April 1940. On the agenda were public shelters and those for domestic use. In the end it was decided that pre-cast concrete trenches were the most practical for the 'floating' population and were provided in strategic locations at the rear of the High Street, near the Town Hall and in Mill Lane, West Watford. Some buildings, like Cassiobury House at the rear of Capel House in Temple Close, were lucky to have their own ready-made shelters in the form of cellars and work was carried out to strengthen domestic basements. According to the *West Herts Post* the first Anderson Shelters arrived in Mildred Avenue and a year later nearly 10,000 had been delivered, a figure that rose to 12,000 shelters for those on an income of £5 per week or less, at a cost to the local rates of £10,000. ARP provision would prove a burden on the rates coupled with the War Budget of 1939 that introduced the country's highest rate of income tax. Adverts in the local press informed readers that air raid shelters and warden's posts could be purchased for £7 10s each from the Standard Range Foundry in Watford. Offices, works, shops and public buildings, such as schools had their own shelters. The importance of the work carried out by the London, Midland & Scottish Railway Company at The Grove meant an extensive network of concrete air raid shelters was built in the grounds. The centre for the coordination of the air raid precautions and the emergency

Newspaper adverts for the Home Guard and air raid shelters, 1940 (Bushey Museum)

services was underground near the Town Hall, its eighteen telephones manned day and night by volunteers. In Northwood coordination was carried out in an old bakery and Rickmansworth had their centre next to the council offices.

The first immediately striking consequence of the war on the area was the sudden influx of evacuees. The government's plan to evacuate threatened urban areas was put into action immediately, and straight away groups from north London and Middlesex appeared in Watford for distribution into rural areas. 'Operation Pied Piper' commenced on 1 September and half-a-million people from the London area were evacuated over four days with an estimated 30,000 children passing through Watford in three days. Though the evacuees were mostly children, there were also mothers, blind persons, disabled children and hospital patients to be dispersed to safe residences and hospitals. In a reverse move, the boys of the London Orphan School in Watford, newly renamed Reed's School after its founder, were evacuated to Devon and the girls to Northampton. The school buildings were converted for use as a military hospital. Watford Junction became a major transition and dispersal point with masses of lost looking children with identification tags flooding the platform. One such group was the 800 children from Islington, who on the first day had to change trains there on their way to Bletchley. Children were taken to a number of distribution centres within Watford (the Trades

Union Hall in Woodford Road, Durrants School), Chorleywood or Abbots Langley, where they were fed before being sent to live with families in rural Hertfordshire. The novelty of having 'loveable cockneys' in their midst proved a source of amusement to the locals and was commented on in the columns of the *Watford Observer*, but there was a certain amount of adjustment to be made on both sides as the city dwellers got used to country life. The county was earmarked for 84,000 evacuees and the numbers continued to grow when a second wave followed once the bombing actually started.

Towns and villages just outside the Watford and Bushey urban area, although in time they would prove not to be immune from air attack themselves, took in the evacuees. At Croxley Green, in common with other centres, reception and billeting was organised by the local authority. Women's groups such as the WVS or the Women's Institute and sometimes even the Girl Guides were called on for assistance and any family with a spare room would be required to take in an evacuee. Families were paid for what might not be an easy task. The allowance was ten shillings and sixpence (52½p) for one child or eight shillings & sixpence per child for more than one. Whole schools were relocated. Abbots Langley took children from two north London schools and Croxley Green took 600 children from three central London schools plus the headmistress of St Albans School, Holborn. Boxmoor and Hemel Hempstead took in children and bombed-out families from East London; the villages of Chipperfield, Bovingdon, Kings Langley and Flaunden took in over a hundred each and Berkhamsted received nearly 2,000. In Chipperfield the evacuees included pregnant women. The extra children put a strain on schooling. Lessons were taught in double shifts or in converted public buildings, such as the Guildhouse and the Methodist Hall in Croxley Green.

In addition to evacuees, villages and towns in the area were called on to house refugees from central Europe and extra workers were drawn from other parts of the country to work in the war related industries. Housing foreigners could be problematic as a landlady soon found out when she was fined £1 for not keeping a register of 'aliens'. Aliens who were deemed to be a threat to national security, those from countries sympathetic to the enemy, were now 'enemy aliens' and in the first two years about 8,000 were temporarily interned in British camps before being deported to the colonies and the dominions. The local enemy aliens were rounded up and held in Kingham Hall, Watford, under police guard before being sent to temporary internment camps. Foreigners fleeing from the enemy still continued to come in numbers. They needed more than just shelter, so a club for German and Czechoslovak refugees was set up in Clarendon Road, Watford.

Soldiers soon began to pour into the region and they required billets too. Schools, like St Margaret's Girls School in Bushey, which was briefly occupied by the 4th City of London Yeomanry, were often used to house the troops. Giving over your rooms for billets could have its advantages. Christopher

Poster for women volunteers to help the local council or WVS with evacuees (public domain)

Masters, who lived in Durban Road, recalled that when the navy took over his house a telephone was installed the next day. Along with the soldiers and workers, bombed-out families from London were also billeted within the neutral zone in the Watford area. As a consequence of all the upheaval the population of Hertfordshire increased by 150,000 during the war.

Despite the flurry of activity as the country readied itself for the fray, the troops marched off for France amidst an atmosphere of surreal calm. After the long years of tense anticipation, the first months of military inactivity were something of an anti-climax and became known as the 'phoney war'. The rapid fall of Poland was followed by a period of digging-in and stalemate. But while the British Expeditionary Force (BEF) may have thought itself safely encamped in northern France behind the supposedly impregnable defences of the Maginot Line, for those at sea matters were getting more serious. The German navy had begun to threaten British shipping and in December there came the news of the Royal Navy's first victory. Able Seaman Wiseman from Boxmoor was aboard the cruiser HMS *Ajax*, which along with HMS *Exeter* and HMS *Achilles* engaged the German battleship *Graf Spee* at the Battle of the River Plate and won; a significant counter to Hitler's propaganda machine. Lieutenant D. East, a Watford Grammar old boy, was wounded in the encounter.

Far from the sunny south Atlantic, back home, after a glorious July and a mild autumn, the winter of 1939 was the coldest for forty-five years. The Grand Union Canal completely froze over from Birmingham to London. The weather may have been a portent, for the summer calm had been merely the lull before the storm. For the first few months of 1940 life went on almost as normal. After an initial disruption the importance of leisure activities as morale boosters was realised and cinemas and theatres had resumed business under blackout restrictions. Watford's new Town Hall was officially opened in January, and in May the annual carnival took place as usual in Cassiobury Park. But the harsh reality of war was finally about to hit home.

Air Raids and the Blitz

> *I have nothing to offer but blood, toil, tears and sweat*
>   Winston Churchill's inaugural speech as prime minister and
>   leader of the new wartime coalition government, 13 May 1940

In April 1940 the land war had suddenly taken a serious turn. Norway was invaded and then in May the Blitzkrieg powered through Holland and Belgium into France, cutting off the BEF. The only course of action for the beleaguered British and Allied troops was evacuation through the port of Dunkirk. Concern gripped the nation as everyone followed the progress of the troops in the papers. By the end of the month the remnants of the army had been successfully plucked from the beaches, but it was a defeat, and the evidence was for all to see as convoys of ambulances took the wounded from Watford Junction to the local hospitals. In June, as Paris fell to the Germans and the last troops trickled home, it was an anxious time for the waiting families who did not know if their loved ones were alive or dead. It would take some time before news of local servicemen who had been captured filtered back, and sometimes the first news came through the newspapers. The next anticipated step was the invasion of Britain and in response the conscription age was raised to 36.

The Germans began their invasion strategy in July with the Luftwaffe's bombing of airfields and supportive infrastructure. This provoked a spirited RAF response. During the long summer of 1940 the aerial Battle of Britain raged. The vapour trails and dogfights that filled the skies of southern England became one of the abiding images of the war. Censorship limited news of the air raids on Kent and Sussex, but soon enough the people of Watford would experience the realities of war first hand. When the RAF's resistance proved more stubborn than the Germans had envisioned, they were forced to change tack, turning their bombers' offensive onto cities and industrial centres. Part of this new strategy was the targeting of civilian areas to weaken morale. Despite the best efforts of the RAF and the Civil Defence, enemy bombers were able to penetrate into south-west Hertfordshire and the area was to suffer more fatalities than any other part of the county. Hitler's decision to launch day and night raids on industrial cities and ports and in particular London, commonly known as the Blitz, began on 7 September 1940 and lasted through until the end of May 1941.

In the Watford area the relative calm of the preceding year was broken on 27 August when for the first time the air raid sirens sounded their dreaded wail to give warning of the need to make for the nearest shelters. The impact of the first raids was felt from the Manor Estate in Hemel Hempstead in the north, to Moor Park and Rickmansworth in the south, where bombs fell harmlessly on the golf courses. Eastbury Avenue in Northwood, Abbots Langley, Oxhey Woods and Primrose Vale and Barnes Lodge Farm in Kings Langley were hit. In the following

WILLS'S CIGARETTES

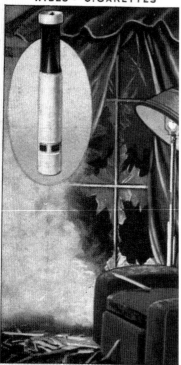
INCENDIARY BOMB AND ITS EFFECT

Advice on how to deal with an incendiary bomb from Wills cigarette cards (Bushey Museum)

days there was a gradual increase of bombs falling on residential areas in and around Watford. The first house to be demolished was in St Albans Road. St Albans Road and Sandringham Road, near to the Greycaines factory, suffered on a number of occasions and the factory was set ablaze by incendiaries. Two houses in Cross Street off Queen's Road and Cawdells department store were damaged and some bombs landed in St Mary's Churchyard and the east window was damaged. The damage at Cawdells was caused by a delayed-action bomb that exploded the next day.

The local papers were not allowed to publish details of bombings at the time in case the information was relayed back to Germany, but as yet there were no serious casualties. On the 12th, the *West Herts Post*, which came out every Thursday, reported a 'big orphanage hit by incendiaries' leaving the Assembly Hall gutted, a reference to damage done to the Royal Caledonian School in Aldenham Road (the hall was rebuilt in 1963). Luckily there were only fifty children in the school at the time – it was still the holidays – and they were quickly hurried to safety in the 'dugouts'. The staff and pupils were evacuated to the Royal Masonic School, an apparently noteworthy occasion for it necessitated the passage of girls through its hallowed portals for the first

House destroyed in Bedswains Lane, Kings Langley, 1941 (Bushey Museum)

time. The following week the paper informed its readers, 'a high explosive bomb, a time bomb and two incendiary bombs were dropped on a large town in S.E. England in the early hours of Monday morning' damaging a street of thirty houses, and there were a number of narrow escapes.

Such escapes would become a feature of people's memories of the raids: when a bomb exploded in the front garden of a house next to the railway line in Gade Avenue, the only damage was a vase blown off the mantelpiece in the front room; after New House Farm in Bovingdon was hit, the fourteen occupants miraculously emerged from the collapsed building without serious injury; and a family in Aldenham escaped unhurt as they slept in the back room of their cottage when a bomb landed at the front. When the first two parachute bombs were dropped one fell in the vicinity of the Royal Masonic School seriously damaging twenty houses in Finch Lane and Avenue Rise,

Clearing up the damage to the Main Hall of the Royal Caledonian School (Bushey Museum)

but there were no casualties. Not everyone was so lucky. By a quirk of fate, an errand boy cycling along Woodland Drive was badly injured when he fell into a crater created by a bomb. He was carried into a nearby house where residents tore up sheets to bind his wounds. One onlooker observed, 'windows were smashed, paving stones were standing upright like tombstones and tiles had been blown off roofs.' In tragic contrast, the first fatalities were in North Watford at 23 Breakespeare Close when three children were killed after an Anderson shelter received a direct hit and a pedestrian was killed nearby in Gammons Lane.

Living in a village was no guarantee of safety from the bombs. Sandwiched between the capital and the industrial towns of the Midlands and close to the industrial and communications targets within Watford and

The bombed-out Bricklayers Arms in Letchmore Heath (Bushey Museum)

the factories and airfields along the route of the Watford Bypass, the rural areas took a significant amount of collateral damage. RAF pilots remarked that Watford from the air contained so many open spaces that it hardly resembled an important industrial centre, as a result more bombs fell in the surrounding fields than on the town itself. This was possibly the result of bombers off-loading their payloads after overshooting their targets or during a hot pursuit by fighters. On the night of 26 September, when the corridor from Tring to Watford was bombed, one bomb landed on the Bricklayers Arms in

Damage to Aldenham Parish Church, October 1940 (Bushey Museum)

Letchmore Heath, killing Laura Jones, the landlady, and Irene Evans aged 15, both remembered on the local war memorial. Unshaken, Major Sir Jocelyn Morton Lucas led the horses and hounds of the Aldenham Hunt past the ruin the next day. The pub was never rebuilt. In time Radlett and Aldenham, where the church tower was damaged, proved to be the worst effected of the outlying villages. On the same night two parachute bombs damaged All Saints Church, the church hall, the Sportsman pub and 358 houses (destroying eight) in Croxley Green. The blast was strong enough to break the window of the Five Shilling Tailors in Rickmansworth High Street a mile away. A few days later Croxley Green suffered again when seven houses in New Road near the Metropolitan Station suffered HE and incendiary damage. That October, in one night houses in Church Lane, Sarratt and Chestnut Avenue, Chorleywood had close calls but the only victims were a haystack and some horses.

In mid-October, the night when Aldenham church was damaged, a hangar at Leavesden airfield had a near miss. It was believed that the reason Aldenham received so much attention was because lorries delivering ammunition for the anti-aircraft batteries at Leavesden would park up overnight in an approach road to the village. At a time of little solid information, rumours passed into folklore. It was said that when the Rose and Crown in Watford was set on fire, in a characteristic exhibition of the bulldog spirit the drinkers carried on regardless. If true, then it would come as no surprise that the considerable damage caused by incendiaries had no effect to the continuation of war work at Ellams Duplicator Company in Bushey. Bushey suffered its most iconic blow on 7 October when the lychgate of St James Church, built to commemorate the fallen of the Great War, was destroyed killing two servicemen who had apparently taken shelter under it. The same blast injured twelve people and damaged stained-glass windows in the church and a number of buildings close by, including the Conservative Club and the Express Dairy. On the 20th, thirteen HE bombs fell in a line from Mill End to Rickmansworth killing two people, demolishing two houses and damaging thirty others. The art and science classrooms were destroyed two days later in Leggatts Way School killing a passing cyclist. The 26th was a heavy night: an HE bomb fell in Cassiobury Park Avenue and incendiaries started a number of fires causing damage to businesses in Watford High Street and killing a bus driver; incendiaries fell on Sarratt, Flaunden and Kings Langley where the proprietor of The Griffin died in his cellar and the pub was destroyed; 16 people were injured and 28 houses damaged in Northwood; and houses in Beechcroft Road, Bushey, were destroyed. On the 28th the Parish Hall of St Mary's and St Matthews Church in Oxhey received a direct hit from a high explosive bomb, tragically killing the seven people sheltering there and damaging the church. The bombs that hit the church and the Oxhey Hall estate were thought to have been meant for the railway at Bushey Arches but the London line remained unscathed. Two bungalows on the St Meryl Estate had to be demolished after being hit by eight HE bombs.

Some of the Luftwaffe pilots did hit their targets. A lone Junkers 88 had carried out an attack on the de Havilland factory at Hatfield on the 3rd destroying the sheet metal shop and halting aircraft production; twenty-seven workers were killed and another seventy injured, many machine-gunned as they ran for the safety of the air-raid shelters. The Junkers was brought down by the airfield's anti-aircraft guns, crashing nearby in Hertingfordbury. And on the final day of the month the main LMS line on the Bushey side of Watford Junction was damaged by an HE bomb. Repair work was carried out immediately and the line was back in action by noon the next day.

In response to the raids, Watford Council circulated a pamphlet with advice on what to do if your house was hit by a bomb:

> *If enemy action has destroyed your home or affected it so that you cannot live in it for the time being, you should go to one of the prepared Rest Centres, at which meals and temporary shelter are provided.*

'German Bomb. Goering's Gift to Bushey. Found 1st April 1941': an unexploded 2,550lb spike-nosed armour-piercing bomb that fell in the garden of Sparrow's Wick, Sparrow's Herne, Bushey, on 14 October 1940 on display in the Victoria Wine shop, Bushey High Street. It sank 40ft into the clay and took six months to dig out (Bushey Museum)

Digging for an unexploded bomb, 1940 (Bushey Museum)

The rest centres were located in schools such as Watford Field School, Victoria School, Garston School, and Parkgate Mixed Primary (now Parkgate Junior School) in Southwold Road.

There had been a number of incidences of unexploded bombs; if this happened people were advised to think about what they might need to take with them and encouraged to 'have a suitcase already packed with essentials in readiness'. If family members became lost or separated they were told to go to the Citizens' Advice Bureau at 14 High Street, Watford. The Council made enough temporary repairs to damaged buildings to enable residents to return home as quickly as possible, leaving the more permanent repairs for later. The Assistance Board Officer was authorized to offer compensation to replace furniture or clothing that had been destroyed and the Council provided free replacement gas masks for those lost or damaged. Employers might also offer help. John Dickinsons & Co turned their Guild of Sport based at Shendish Manor into a home for their bombed-out workers.

If the bombs were not enough there was a further danger of falling anti-aircraft shells from the AA batteries, which could be either mobile or sited within the town and outlying districts. Although the shells were timed to explode in the air, making a distinctive sound that could be heard on the ground, not all went off and on return to earth could cause damage or injury. Stricken planes falling from the skies added another hazard. There were RAF as well as Luftwaffe casualties: the Hurricane or Spitfire that crashed landed near Fortherley Road, Rickmansworth; the Spitfire that came down during a snowstorm on Gammons Lane, Watford; the Spitfire that crashed in farmland in Chipperfield after an engine malfunction; and the Hurricane (possibly) that crashed off Green Street, Chorleywood. The number of crashed aircraft instigated a useful secondary industry of cannibalising and reconstructing new planes from the wreckage, sometimes on the spot. Local workers wearing special jerseys bearing the motto 'Ubend 'um we'll mend 'um' restored almost a plane a day.

When the residents around Chesham ('a Home Counties town' in the *Bucks Examiner* report) found themselves on the receiving end of a 'stick' of six bombs that caused two fatalities, it was thought this was probably the result of a stray bomber getting rid of its load; the target being Bovingdon aerodrome close by. Bovingdon aerodrome was not built yet, so it is surprising that the village was already on the receiving end of a number of bomb drops. Bovingdon is close to the rail and canal route north and it may be more likely it was from a bomber that had missed its target somewhere along the route. Reporting restrictions meant the news of raids was imprecise in contemporary reports, giving little indication of time, location or damage. Residents' memories are often equally vague and rumour might fill the gaps. A typical announcement in the *Watford Observer* (11 October 1940) read, 'A high explosive bomb dropped in a densely populated area of a South-Eastern town in the early hours of Friday caused the death of an old age pensioner – Mr. Samuel Frederick Circuit, aged 70.' The report gave the street name and with this information and the resident's name it is possible to locate the address in Watford as 13 Souldern Street. The *West Herts Post* (24 October) reported the first daylight raid on the town during which Woodland Drive was hit and as the dogfights took place overhead machine-gun bullets fell on the road. Even though foreign radio stations may have inaccurately reported Watford and St Albans being bombed on 28 October it probably mattered little as again the *West Herts Post* three days later carried the story of eighty incendiaries raining down on the shopping centre of a 'town in the home counties' with bombs rolling off the Town Hall roof.

No one needed newspapers or radios to be aware of the Blitz on London. When in November the bombing raids changed to night attacks, the sound of the explosions that could be heard as far as Watford was accompanied by a clearly visible red glow in the sky as the city burned; a horrifying sight for those who watched mesmerized from vantage points on high ground such as West Herts Golf Course or Chorleywood Common. Each night searchlight beams were visible scouring the skies and the sound of anti-aircraft guns could be heard from over the Vauxhall plant in Luton to the north, where tanks were being made, to London to the south. People lucky enough to have a car sought refuge at night from the worst bombed urban areas in the relative quiet of the countryside as far afield as Chipperfield Common. During the daylight raids, watchers below cheered on their brave Spitfire pilots locked in a life and death struggle with an enemy bomber.

During November the bombing continued unabated. Houses were destroyed in Abbots Langley and Cassiobury Park Avenue. The quarters of the nuns at Rosary Priory, adjacent to the girl's convent school in Caldecote Towers in Elstree Road, Bushey, took a direct hit. The severity of the blast was enough to damage other houses in the road. The school was being used as a WAAF hostel, but, some thought miraculously, there were only five minor injuries. HEs caused casualties in Hillcroft Crescent, Oxhey, Tudor

*Bomb damage to the electricity supply offices in St John's Road, Watford, 1940
(Bushey Museum)*

Avenue and Sandringham Road, Watford, and Hazelwood Lane and Gallows Hill, Abbots Langley. On 16 November a bomb landed near Rickmansworth Gas Works; a gas main was hit and two men, a woman and a child were killed. Captain Fairman, the chief constable of Hertfordshire, decided to check the blackout precautions by flying over the county during a raid and possibly rightly the council concluded that they were not efficient enough as at the end of the month 200 incendiary bombs fell on the town in one

Bomb damage to Rosemary Priory and Caldecote Towers (Bushey Museum)

night. The town centre suffered most damage from incendiaries while the outer core was mainly on the receiving end of high explosive bombs. St Johns Road was hit on 4 December killing five including two children, and two nights later two adults and two children were killed in Eastlea Avenue after a bomber was hit by fire from the Munden Drive battery and jettisoned its bombs. It came down in Lord Knutsford's Munden estate near Brickett Wood, hitting a tree and killing all the crew and the occupants of the house adjacent. Watford suffered 23 fatalities between 22 September and 9 December. There were 29 alerts in December and one lasted 13 hours and 47 minutes, the longest of the war.

In the new year the pattern continued. It began with cluster bombs dropped between Nascott Wood Road and the Ridgeway and the next night the toy department at Trewins in Queen's Road was damaged by incendiaries and the Mount Zion Church and the Wall Paper Company were set on fire. Targeting the town centre may have been deliberate, but apart from some damage in areas near manufacturing activity in West Watford, off St Albans Road or to the north of North Western Avenue, it is unclear if any damage was the result of deliberate identification or merely the result of indiscriminate action. In general the bombers seem to have had little success in hitting their targets, with most of their bombs falling on residential areas or open spaces. After the war it was revealed that the Town Hall had been designated an industrial target by the enemy, but that remained untouched too. Despite this more bombs fell in the rural areas of the county. If the bombers were coming back from targets in the Midlands, such as Coventry, they would empty their remaining load along the Gade valley in the hope of hitting the canal, the main road (A41) and the railway lines to disrupt munitions and supplies coming from Birmingham through to the docks. The Ovaltine factory that made rations and Dickinsons paper mill where mortar bombs were made were also targets. They did manage a strike when Aldenham aerodrome was hit that January but again the bombs mainly fell in Radlett Road and Balmoral Road causing some damage to Reed's School and at the end of the month on Park Avenue.

Eventually bombings would become so much a part of everyday life that people could set their watches by the raids and as the war progressed children playing in the fields around Watford and the surrounding villages would increasingly stumble across bomb craters, and sometimes their morbid curiosity would be aroused by gruesome remains and debris from explosions. By February the bombing began to slow, and by March 1941 the Blitz was over. But the danger was not over; sporadic air raids continued, if not as intensely. And there were still fatalities; in Maple Cross in April and then at Nash Mills in May – when three HEs killed two wardens, four male and two female evacuees and a child, damaged 150 houses and made 50 people homeless.

Indefatigable spirit: Guy dressed as Hitler with toothbrush moustache and swastika on top of a bonfire (Bushey Museum)

Shortages and rationing

Aerial attack was not the only way Britain could be weakened prior to invasion. Britain's vulnerability was its dependence on imports and shipping, and as in the First World War German strategy was to deploy U-boats to cut supply routes in the Atlantic. Once the Germans had the Continental Atlantic ports under their control the Axis navies were in a position to completely starve Britain of materials and food. The U-boat commanders referred to the summer of 1940 as 'the happy time' as it marked a particularly successful period in their attempts to disrupt allied merchant shipping during what became known as the Battle of the Atlantic. One Watford casualty of the U-boats was Seaman Jack King of Elfrida Road. Eighteen-year-old Jack was torpedoed while serving as a deck hand on the SS *African Star*. He survived the attack but was held as a PoW until he was repatriated in 1943. What Churchill called the 'U-boat peril' lasted throughout the war, but these were particularly dark days when the future of the nation hung in the balance. The extra material demands of militarization combined with the blockade meant shortages were inevitable. To deal with the shortfall in aircraft supply, in May Churchill's new coalition government appointed the press baron and owner of the *Daily Express* Max Aitken (Lord Beaverbrook) as Minister of Aircraft Production. Beaverbrook's rapid impact saw an increase in production that sucked in materials, so in July, as a propaganda exercise, he launched an appeal for public donations that could 'turn your pots and pans into Spitfires and Hurricanes, Blenheims and Wellingtons.' In response cooking utensils and household implements came flooding in, providing over 70,000 tons of aluminium for recycling, particularly into aircraft.

Heavier raw materials like iron and steel were needed for munitions and in addition to the collection of scrap metal in 1941 the government began compulsorily requisitioning all iron gates and railings installed after 1850. Workmen removing railings and iron gates from people's front gardens or from outside commercial buildings became a common sight. In Croxley Green the disappearing railings included the original cattle guards from around the commemorative trees and the War Memorial on the Green. A few exceptions were made for items of particular historic interest, usually elaborate gates. The intended requisitioning of the fencing that enclosed Dickinsons sports field, where the pavilion had been taken over as a children's nursery, and the new ornamental gates caused an outcry and they were only saved after protests and letters to the Ministry from mothers concerned for the safety of their children. As the need for raw materials became even more acute, children proved adept at the job of salvaging anything of worth. Alan Orchard, who lived in Kingswood, remembered that the children would take their 'carts and old prams' and

> ... knock on doors to ask for "scrap", taking the resulting jam jars, beer bottles, newspapers, old cooking pots and pans, rags, bones and scrap metal to the jam factory, brewery, West Herts Post or down to the scrap merchants at the bottom of the High Street.

They received a welcome 'very few coppers' in return for their trouble. Recycling would continue through the war. To counter paper shortages publications as various as newspapers and theatre programmes were reduced in size and from 1942 the collection of waste paper and books for 'salvage' was encouraged.

One thing that affected everyone was food rationing. To ensure food supplies could be maintained, it was necessary to control stocks and prices. This responsibility fell to a wartime-only Ministry of Food, a separate department from the Ministry of Agriculture. Petrol had been rationed from the outset, but as the situation worsened, on 8 January 1940 bacon, butter and sugar were rationed, followed by meat, tea, jam and preserves, biscuits, breakfast cereals, cheese, eggs, lard, milk, canned and dried fruit, and sweets. Everyone was required to have a national registration number, ration card and a ration book with coupons to exchange for goods in the shops. Lord Woolton took over as minister in April 1940 as the shortages began to bite, and introduced point rationing and feeding stations. Locally a food control committee was formed at Chater Junior School in Addiscombe Road, and it was here that around 68,000 ration cards were produced and 1,100 food retailers licensed. Fish and fresh fruit and vegetables were not rationed. The quantities varied slightly during the war but the minimum average weekly ration was

3 pints of milk

8 oz sugar

2 oz butter

4 oz margarine

3 oz lard

3 oz cheese

4 oz bacon and ham

1s 2d (equivalent to £2.90 in 2018) worth of meat (went down to 1s in May 1941)

1 egg (when available) or one packet of egg powder (per month)

2 oz sweets

2 oz preserves

2 oz tea

Offal and sausages were rationed between 1942 and 1944; sausages contained very little meat when they were not rationed. There was flexibility: vegetarians could supplement other foods for meat; extra milk, cod liver oil and orange juice were available for babies, young children and expectant and nursing mothers. Paradoxically, food rationing in general, and particularly for the poor, had a beneficial effect on diet and the reduction of tooth decay by ensuring a balanced intake and cutting sweet and fatty foods. Restrictions on food and certain goods were too much for some people and the inevitable black market trade meant there were a number of cases of individuals being caught and fined for possessing large quantities of rationed items. A notorious incident was when a Bovingdon woman was discovered in her Rolls Royce with enough sugar rations for 140 people for which she had paid over £2. She was fined £90 and the greengrocer £170; at the time an Austin saloon cost £128.

The Ministry of Food initiated a programme to educate the public in nutrition and encouraged the growing of vegetables, particularly carrots and potatoes (with the aid of cartoon characters Potato Pete and Dr Carrot)

Dig for Victory poster by Scottish cartoonist Peter Fraser (public domain)

through its 'Dig for Victory' campaign. A 'Woolton pie' was a pastry or potato crust filled with carrots, parsnips, potatoes and turnips in oatmeal topped with brown gravy. To supply the demand for vegetables any available land, beside railway tracks or in parks and gardens, was turned over to growing foodstuffs. The land bought for the extension of the Northern line to Bushey Heath was given over to allotments and one of the uses of the large available spaces of Cassiobury Park was for the same purpose. Watford Council had purchased Leggatts Farm for building, but at the end of 1940, along with Harwoods Recreation Ground, it was given over to allotments. The young were encouraged to get involved. The pupils of Victoria Senior School, then situated in Addiscombe Road, were taken to tend the school allotments at King Georges Avenue and Cassiobury Park. Out of the town, the boys of Aldenham School were put to helping the farmers with general tasks, picking potatoes, planting onions, herding cattle and local children helped with the harvest. The keeping of animals that could be easily looked after was encouraged. Waste food and scraps were put aside to feed pigs. Dustmen made collections and there were large galvanised bins for the feed placed in the streets. The council kept pigs on their farm at Holywell and encouraged people to form their own

Sheep grazing on Bushey Hall golf course, 1944 (Bushey Museum)

pig clubs. Pigs were kept on West Herts Golf Course, there was a pig club in Green Lane, Oxhey, and the members of Bushey Hall Golf Club formed their own, using the swill from the hotel kitchens for feed. To complement the egg ration, some people took to keeping chickens. As a sideline there was a black market trade in eggs.

It was not until June 1941 that clothing began to be rationed, and famously nylon stockings became unavailable. Because clothing coupons never went far enough the Ministry of Information issued a pamphlet entitled 'Make Do and Mend' which became a memorable catch phrase. In its largely successful attempt to foster a culture in which nothing was thrown away, it provided thrifty design ideas and advice on how to reuse old clothing so that housewives could be frugal and stylish at the same time. The production of non-essential civilian items was halted completely by 1942 and even the supply of furniture was limited. In July 1942 the basic civilian petrol ration was abolished, leaving fuel only available for priority use; the emergency services, transport, farmers and of course the military.

The shortages had some unexpected upbeat outcomes. As a result of the huge increase in barley growing during the war, Colonel W.H. Briggs, the chairman of Benskin's Brewery, noted in the company report published in the *Brewing Trade Review* (1950) the company's continued success despite the restrictions and the reduction in the quantity and strength of the beer brewed. It was the first time since the 1840s that the industry was using exclusively British ingredients and there was an ample supply of local barley and hops.

CHAPTER SIX

Warriors for the Working Day

For the first time in its history, the country experienced total war. There was virtually no aspect of life immune from the war effort, either in work or play. Adapting Shakespeare's *Henry V*, everyone was now a warrior on a daily basis.

Life goes on

For morale it was important that life retained as much of an air of normality as was possible. Leisure activities provided vital distractions from everyday concerns and in the summer local fetes and carnivals continued to be held. Today's big distraction, TV, was still in its infancy. Regular BBC broadcasts from Alexandra Palace had only been in existence for three years, so its suspension for the duration of the war until its resumption in 1946 was only bad news for the few (about 40,000 homes) lucky enough to own a TV set. In 1939 the means of escapism for most people was cinema. It was a year of iconic movies (*Wuthering Heights*, *The Wizard of Oz*, *Goodbye, Mr Chips*, *Gone with the Wind*) and attendance was booming with many people going more than once a week, so one can imagine the reaction when the government closed cinemas and theatres in the first week of the war; only to reverse the decision straight away when they realized it would be more advantageous to keep them open. Apart from entertainment, cinemas provided an outlet for propaganda and films tailor-made as morale boosters. The classic morale booster came later in 1944 – Laurence Olivier's version of *Henry V* made to coincide with the Normandy landings. The entertainment put on at cinemas, as long as it conformed to blackout regulations, was adaptable. The stages could be used for music as well as films, so big bands performed at the Odeon, and the new Gaumont with its Wurlitzer organ hosted shows in the style of Sydney Kaplan and his Music Hall Orchestra. Most cinemas and theatres escaped the bombing, but the Gaumont suffered fire damage in 1943. The roof was discovered to be aflame in the interval after a trailer for the ominously named film *So Ends Our Night* had been shown, terminating the evening's musical entertainment. The cinema had to be closed, but the damage was slight enough for it to open again early the following year.

At the end of August 1939 the young Michael Aldridge, who went on to have a successful acting career (*Tinker, Tailor, Soldier, Spy*; *Last of the*

Summer Wine), was making his interrupted professional debut at Watford's Palace Theatre in *French without Tears* by Terence Rattigan; a year later he was in the RAF. Once the theatres were reopened, theatre-goers were confronted with the following ARP notice:

> *You will be notified from the stage if an air raid warning has been given during the performance. This does not mean that an air raid will take place. If you wish to leave the Theatre you are at will to do so, but if you must go, all we ask is that you depart quietly and without excitement.*
>
> *Don't forget your gas mask.*

Apparently this did not put audiences off. In addition to the resumed weekly repertory performances, the manager, Andrew Melville, continued to put on the annual Christmas pantomimes, including *Queen of Hearts* (1940) and *Dick Whittington* (1942). Concerts were held in the new Watford Town Hall. Here the fleet-of-foot could enjoy the well-known dance bands and orchestras of Jack Payne, Mantovani, Sydney Kyte, Jack Jackson and Eddie Carroll (who became an officer in the army in 1941). For the more sedate, there was the London Philharmonic Orchestra, which did extensive tours of the country during the war and played there under Malcolm Sargent. As well as the famous names, there were local regional bands doing the rounds in the county, such as Ken 'Jive' Bedford, Percy Rance and his 'full broadcasting orchestra' and Reg Heckford and the Five Rhythmists, whose adverts reveal they were available for hire for dances.

Cinema and theatre may have been able to make the best of a difficult situation, but competitive sport was badly disrupted. The threat of air attack and the introduction of conscription, which took the young and the fit, made it impossible for football to continue as before. When the 1939-40 football season was suspended after three matches, Watford FC was lying a lowly 17th out of 22 teams in League Division 3 (South), having not yet won a game. Reading and Crystal Palace were the league leaders. On 21 September the Home Office had a rethink following general protest and, taking the effect on morale into account, decided to permit the implementation of a revised football programme as long as it did not interfere with national service and industry. Many league players were called up into the forces or drafted into war work. Joe Coen, a Scottish professional who played for Luton Town, was killed while serving with the RAF and Arsenal lost three of their players on active service. With so many players missing, teams fielded numerous 'guests', usually players serving nearby, and amateurs. One roving professional was Albert Bonass who was officially on Queens Park Rangers' books. While serving in the RAF, Bonass played for a number of clubs including Watford. He was killed in 1945 when his Stirling bomber crashed killing all the crew and a civilian.

With travel restricted, ten regional mini-leagues were formed and the FA Cup was replaced with a limited Football League War Cup. Home internationals and inter-service matches added interest to the fixture lists. As a result, despite grounds being badly affected by air raid damage, changes of use and general disruption, football remained a popular spectator sport. Crowds were limited to 8,000 in evacuation areas and 15,000 elsewhere. Watford played in two leagues of ten teams, South A and D, finishing fourth behind Arsenal and West Ham and third behind Crystal Palace and QPR at the end of the season. During the Blitz, the traditional ban on Sunday games was lifted to give factory workers a respite and on Christmas Day 1940, Watford played Luton home and away, drawing 2-2 in the morning at Vicarage Road and then losing 4-1 at Kenilworth Road in the afternoon. The 1940-1 season saw the leagues being reduced to only two, a North (34 teams) and South (36 teams) regional championship, with limited matches being organized by accessibility rather than status. Watford played 35 matches whereas Coventry and Swansea only played 10. The winner was decided on goal average, with Crystal Palace coming out on top over 27 games. Watford came eighth.

During the war Aldershot, the army town, did very well thanks to its high number of guest players, many of whom were peacetime internationals such as Matt Busby, Joe Mercer, Tommy Lawton and Frank Swift. To add to the confusion there was also a Football League South with the champions decided on their average score. For those for whom this was not enough, there were the friendly matches against the service teams, such as the Royal Army Medical Corps and the Royal Army Service Corps. The latter was interrupted by an air raid warning seven minutes into its match with Watford and the game was abandoned half an hour later when the Army team was recalled to duty. Interruption due to air raids would prove to be a common occurrence considerably extending match times. In 1941-2 the leagues were reorganized again, with 16 teams forming a London League playing 30 matches. Watford, who used a record 83 players, found this competition tougher, finishing bottom. In one match Fred Kurtz of Grimsby Town, who was stationed at Woolwich Arsenal, played under the alias 'Newman' to cover the fact that he was Absent Without Leave. The next season the 'London' teams returned to the Football League South and in the final 1944-5 season Watford climbed to a creditable tenth.

Sport was a vital recreation. In all three services, football was encouraged as a way to keep troops fit, active and entertained and many factories set up male and female football teams. Prisoners of war on both sides of the conflict were encouraged to play and footballs and kit were sent out to prison camps by the Red Cross and the YMCA. Cricket was more severely disrupted than football with first class matches and test cricket being abandoned. Cricket grounds were perceived to be too dangerous and some were closed or requisitioned. In an effort to keep the game going, charity and inter-service games were played and reduced fixtures continued at local clubs. Other sports were not so affected. In March 1940, a Wednesday evening boxing match between Jack Millburn, the Bletchley and Leighton middleweight, and the Watford local boy Reg Hunt was reckoned important enough to be broadcast on a 'Forces' radio programme. Milburn won on points over six rounds. The following May, Milburn was back in Watford taking on Cash Hawkins of Battersea, whom he defeated at the cost of a fractured hand.

Saving for the War and events to raise money

In many ways saving and raising funds became a form of diversion and became closely interwoven into leisure activities. Saving schemes had been an established government method of offsetting the shortfall in money raised through taxation for public spending since 1916. After the hard interwar years, by 1939 Britain was still in no position to finance a war and the government was forced to appeal to the nation not only to tighten its belt but also to actively fund the war effort. A War Savings Campaign was launched to promote the buying of Defence Bonds and in response local savings groups were formed. School groups and groups of people living in the same street proved particularly successful. Other saving schemes included paying cash into government accounts such as War Bonds, Savings Bonds, and Savings Certificates through the Post Office or at banks. Posters carrying snappy slogans like 'Lend to Defend the Right to be Free', 'Save your way to Victory' and 'War Savings are Warships', promoted local savings weeks. Only part of the money saved was through the efforts of ordinary people; their contributions were boosted with donations from banks, insurance companies and local firms.

The first crisis to deal with was the stretched resources of the RAF. During the Battle of Britain their reserves were taken to breaking point, with pilots and planes in short supply. Lord Beaverbrook, as Minister for Aircraft Production, had so dramatically turned round the urgent replacement of machines that Churchill acknowledged the improvement in a letter to the Secretary of State for Air (June 1940) saying that he had cleared up 'the muddle and scandal of the aircraft production branch'. To make these improvements Beaverbrook required not only men and materials but also money. As a newspaperman, he instinctively realised the potentially iconic status of the Spitfire and he hyped up its image and that of its pilots so that it became synonymous with the RAF's success. As a result, unsolicited donations came flooding in to help in the plane's manufacture. Encouraged by these local initiatives based around household collections and events, he rolled out the initiative into a nationwide campaign. As a reward for an individual, a town, or a company raising £5,000, a 'Presentation Spitfire' would be emblazoned with the name of the donor. To spur on the donors of Watford during the 'Spitfire for Victory' campaign, a Messerschmitt 109 that had been shot down and salvaged from a Sussex cornfield was exhibited behind the Cawdells store in the High Street. Even so, the Watford fund only just reached its target in time for Spitfire W3456 to bear the name of the town in four-inch high yellow letters on its fuselage. 'Watford' did not survive the war, coming to a sad end in 1944 when its Turkish pilot, Hudai Toros, crashed near Cranwell. The £5,000 figure was in reality a nominal sum, being only enough to pay for the plane's fuselage. The total construction cost was £8,000 to £12,000 (about £400,000 to £500,000 in current terms). Eventually the national total raised, collected from donations that ranged from children's pocket money to thousands of pounds, came to about £13 million. Apparently not everyone was prepared to put the war effort before other sentiments. When a Messerschmitt, perhaps the same one, was displayed outside St James's Church in Bushey in June 1941, the positioning of the enemy plane on the village green caused a rumpus. It was thought in bad taste and the land had been donated on the understanding that nothing was to be erected on it. The *Watford Observer* reported that at the Bushey Council meeting Mr Dale expressed his feeling of shame regarding the attitude of members of the community stating that the Messerschmitt may have blotted out the view of the church but 'if we had no Spitfires the Church would not be blotted out, but blasted out'. The council decided to ignore the complaints of the protesters.

Following on from the success of the Spitfire campaign further savings and fund-raising campaigns were launched. To replace the devastating loss of military equipment abandoned on the beach at Dunkirk there was 'a War Weapons Week' held in May 1941. In Watford a biplane was displayed by The Parade and model warships sailed on the Pond. This must have helped, for the town's target figure of £250,000 was easily surpassed; in the event £1,272,629 was raised! To give added impetus to the efforts of such 'Special Weeks', spectacular displays were mounted and competition encouraged between towns. In 1942, Watford was put in competition with Luton, Luton Rural District and Dunstable combined. During 'Warships Week', £1,225,809 was raised, but it was pipped by Luton and company who raised £1,421,714. In February, Bushey managed £120,000 for the fund from a population of 12,000; this at a time when, as Tom Harrison reported in the *Spectator* (20 March 1942), over two-thirds of munitions workers earned less than £4 pounds a week. The money paid for HMS *Woodpecker*, a Black Swan Class sloop launched on 29 June. Used in convoy defence, it successfully performed anti-submarine duties and was credited with sinking six U-boats until it fell victim to a torpedo in 1944. The crew had built strong links with Bushey where a Woodpecker Contact Committee had been formed. Among other things they sent knitted socks and jerseys to the crew. The first survivor to be picked up from the stricken ship was its mascot, 'Bushey' the ship's cat. In 1945, members of the crew were entertained in Falconers Hall, and years later

BUSHEY & BUSHEY HEATH have set as their Warship Week objective £120,000 — to adopt the Corvette *Heliotrope*. The men of this gallant warship are doing their job by risking their lives—*you* can help them to win through by SAVING for all you're worth during WARSHIP WEEK. Fight the U-Boats from your own fireside with a family salvo of War Savings! H.M.S. *Heliotrope* is looking to you!

Go to one of the special selling centres, a Post Office, or your Bank or Stockbroker and invest your money in 3% Savings Bonds 1955-65, 2¼% National War Bonds 1949-51, 3% Defence Bonds, or Savings Certificates : or deposit your savings in the Post Office Savings Bank. Buy Savings Stamps at 6d. and 2/6d. each, from a Post Office or your Savings Group.

INVEST ALL YOU CAN IN THESE

3% Savings Bonds

2½% National War Bonds

3% Defence Bonds

Savings Certificates

Post Office Savings Bank

GRAND MARCH PAST Saturday, Feb. 21st, 2.30 p.m. 8 bands and a Bigger and Better Show than ever! Roll up and cheer this demonstration of British and Allied might!

BUSHEY & BUSHEY HEATH WARSHIP WEEK FEB. 21-28

Save for "all you're Worth"

survivors held a reunion in Bushey in 1995. Watford's adopted ship was HMS *Capetown*, a 'C' class cruiser launched in 1918. It had already seen service in the Mediterranean and the Indian Ocean and went on to take part in the Normandy landings. Hemel Hempstead's adopted ship, the Hunt class destroyer HMS *Berkeley*, was not so lucky. Commissioned in 1940, it took part as an escort in the infamous raid on Dieppe in August 1942 and after being hit by two bombs, killing thirteen ratings, it had to be scuttled.

Further fund raisers followed: the band of the Irish Guards, stationed at Northwood, made an appearance in Watford in support of another War Weapons Week; 'Tanks for Attack', a Ministry of Information exhibition that toured local museums, made a visit; in May 1943 'Wings for Victory Week' featured a veteran Lancaster bomber assembled outside the Town Hall (the target was £1,000,000 to build fifty Mosquitos; it was exceeded by £150,326); 'Salute the Soldier Week', another travelling exhibition (1944); and finally Thanksgiving Week (1945) to help in the return of 'our boys' from overseas duty. To celebrate victory, Dickinsons ran a special Thanksgiving Savings Week edition of the company paper.

'Fight the U-Boats from your own fireside' – newspaper advertisement for Warships Week, February 1942. The money raised was to have been for the corvette HMS Heliotrope *but in the event the ship was leant to the US navy (as USS* Surprise*) and Bushey's donation went to HMS* Woodpecker *instead (Bushey Museum)*

Firms such as Dickinsons had supported fundraising efforts and the proceeds from *Dickinsons News* went towards a Troops Comforts Fund. A.G. Symmons, the director of Sun Engravings, was an energetic gardener and he turned his efforts to growing fruit and vegetables on a more massive scale. Besides giving plants to others to encourage them to grow their own food, he also staged exhibits of his produce to raise money for the Sun's Forces Fund, the Red Cross, and local charities. In November 1944, Sun Engraving began their own Light Orchestra, and their first performances at the Old Merchant Taylors' Home, the Peace Memorial Hospital and in the works' canteen proved such successes that the management arranged for the orchestra to put on a show at the Palace Theatre in aid of the British Red Cross P.O.W. Fund. To underline the link between entertainment and fund raising, an advertisement from March 1942 read, 'Coming to Cawdells, Chessington famous Dog and Monkey Circus for One Week… dogs, monkey and tiny pony plus a surprise, proceeds to Peace Memorial Hospital.' The event was a popular success and returned in November.

Working for the war effort

The most direct way civilians could contribute to the war effort was through their work. Reserved occupations in manufacturing, the railways and docks, mining and agriculture exempted skilled workers from being called up into the forces. Despite this many industries suffered staff shortages. At Sun Engravers almost half the male staff were called away (over 1,000 employees) to serve in the forces, and at John Dickinson and Co, after the company had initially cooperated with the recruitment services in allowing staff to join the Territorial Army where possible, when work in the paper industry became included in the number of reserved occupations, there was a reluctance to grant permission to join up. For those married men with dependents who had joined the forces, Dickinsons paid an allowance to their families and employees made occasional home visits to make sure all was well. As in the First World War, women stepped in for the men, and there were numerous vacancies to be filled in all manner of occupations. From the start, the telephone and fire alarm systems in Watford fire station were manned by women, while other women trained to drive the borough's ambulances which were based at the first-aid HQ behind the public baths in Hempstead Road. Once again young female school leavers were expected to take on war work in the factory, on the farm, or even in the shops.

In the surrounding rural countryside there were opportunities for women to work in the Women's Land Army. The call to arms meant that initially there was an acute shortage of agricultural labour. To begin with a choice was given between joining the forces or the WLA, and girls with farm experience might choose the latter. Most of the women though came from the cities, particularly

Land Girls in the packing shed at Rochford's Nurseries in Turnford near Broxbourne c. 1943 and (opposite page) Molly Clarke's (back row right) Land Army pledge (Both from the Bushey Museum)

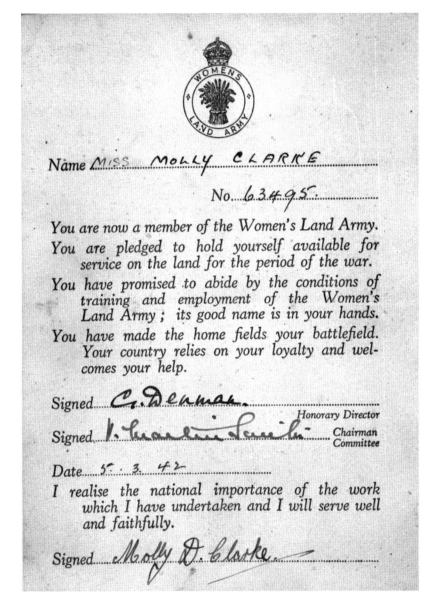

Name *Miss Molly Clarke*

No. *63495*.

You are now a member of the Women's Land Army.
You are pledged to hold yourself available for
service on the land for the period of the war.
You have promised to abide by the conditions of
training and employment of the Women's
Land Army; its good name is in your hands.
You have made the home fields your battlefield.
Your country relies on your loyalty and wel-
comes your help.

Signed .... *Honorary Director*

Signed .... *Chairman*
Committee

Date ..... *5 . 3 . 42* .....

I realise the national importance of the work
which I have undertaken and I will serve well
and faithfully.

Signed ..... *Molly D. Clarke* .....

London, and had little idea of what farm work involved. The reality of fifty
hours or so of arduous labour starting around 6.30 in the morning, paid at
22s 6d per week (increased to 48s in 1944), was a far cry from the romantic
pastoral idyll portrayed on the recruitment posters. But the posters must have
done their job: in 1939 there were only 65 women working on the land in

Recruitment poster for the Women's Land Army (public domain)

Hertfordshire, but by 1943 there were over 2,100 and many of them found it a rewarding experience.

Park Farm claimed to be the first to use Land Girls in the county. The largest local agricultural recruiter was Ovaltine, which had farms in King's Langley and Abbots Langley where the Land Girls worked as milkmaids and as general helpers. Large houses and estates, such as Pendley Manor near Tring, were ideal for housing and employing the WLA, and Little Gaddesden near Ashridge had thirty-four girls from Yorkshire billeted there. In King's Langley, Barnes House (now demolished) was requisitioned and used as a hostel as well as for its other secret 'war work' and in Abbots Langley the Queen Anne style Serge Hill House, the centre of an estate with a number of farms, and Pimlico House in Hyde Lane, were used as WLA hostels. There were even land girls billeted at West Herts Golf Club where their presence in the Club House was said to have distracted many a golfer making a vital putt on the 18th hole. On smaller farms the girls were normally billeted with the farmer's family. As the war progressed the land girls might find they were working alongside German PoWs who had been be drafted in to help, but fraternisation was not encouraged. The smaller farms in Bushey, Highfield Farm and Coldharbour Farm, employed land girls; the latter, after a bit of deliberation, taking two in preference to having a PoW staying at the farm.

When the War Agricultural Executive Committee commandeered tracts of The Grove estate's available land to grow wheat and other crops, the WLA

Group of PoWs working on Hedges' farm bringing in the hay, 1945 (Bushey Museum)

were initially brought in to undertake much of the work. The Grove estate was occupied by the London, Midland & Scottish Railway and most of the railway staff became involved in the running of the farm, usually during the summer months when they were co-opted into haymaking. Some members of the estate department were sent on a concentrated farming course at Oaklands Agricultural College in St Albans before returning as farm managers. After a time the WLA were replaced by German and Italian PoWs who proved to be good workers and caused no trouble, always willing to pass the time of day and getting on well with members of the railway staff.

The urgent need for machines and ordnance for the forces turned manufacturing almost completely into a militarised economy. With a depleted workforce it was necessary to draft women into the factories and in March 1941 women began to be called up for war work, deployed as engineers or drivers, including tanks, or working in munitions factories or as nurses. In December, national service was introduced for all unmarried women between the ages of 20 and 30. By mid-1943, 90 per cent of single women and 80 per cent of married women were employed in the armed forces or in industry; this meant that it was mainly women who were building the Mosquito aircraft at Leavesden aerodrome.

These demands created a problem for married women at a time when childcare was scarce, so provisions had to be made to free up women with young children for work. As the factories in north Watford and along the Bypass were important employers, a Day Nursery was built in Briar Road, Garston, for this purpose. Food centres that had initially been set up to feed bombed-out families were also used for children whose parents were working. The Ministry of Food established centres at Watford Field School, Sotherton Road School, Chalk Hill School, Parkgate School, Victoria School, and at the Town Hall. Out of Watford there were centres in Chipperfield in the Women's Club Room and King's Langley in Rucklers Lane Hall. Even so, however many women were employed they could not fulfill all the requirements of war work. For specialist jobs, workers had to be drafted in from elsewhere. As a result, local households who had the space might find they were required by the government to take in an engineer and his family, as in one instance of an engineer from Kent who came to work at Savage and Parsons.

The light engineering that had contributed to the growth of Watford and the surrounding area was well placed to supply the increased military needs. A number of local firms and occupations were given over entirely to military purposes, others only in part. Versatility was an important requirement, and produced some surprising results. For example, the top floor of British Moulded Hose in Sandown Road, Watford, was turned over to the manufacture of penicillin. The Official Secrets Act covered much of what went on in the factories engaged in the war effort so their work was largely unknown to outsiders. Some of the unusual activities were more secret than others. In West Watford, the premises of Allensor, who were joiners in King Gregory Avenue, became the site of SOE station VIIc Wireless Section Research. Station VIIb Wireless Section, located nearby in the Yeast-Vite factory in Whippendell Road, was employed in research, packing and dispatch. In normal times Yeastvite were makers of foodstuffs, and neither had any previous experience of wireless. An atmosphere of the utmost secrecy enveloped their neighbours, Watford Electric and Manufacturing Company (later Wemco), who manufactured switchgear for the Royal Navy. When the threat of invasion was at its height, to safeguard their top-secret plans a reliable courier would be entrusted to take copies to a prearranged meeting point where they were handed over to a government agent for shipping to the USA for safekeeping. Cox & Co, a company with experience in vehicle manufacture, were commissioned by the government to carry out the slightly less clandestine work of producing decoy tanks made of tubular steel and canvas. Similarly, Chiswell Wire Company was put to work making bayonets.

Grace's Guide to Industry informs us that in 1939 Savage and Parsons Ltd, on Watford Bypass (an offshoot of CA Parsons the big turbine engineers in Newcastle upon Tyne) were already supplying to the aircraft industry. Major John Clifford ('Mad Jack') Savage MBE was an aviation and engineering pioneer who had served in the RAF in the First World War. In *Grace's* words the company made a 'sound locator trainer' that provided

> ...a rapid and economical means of training sound locator personnel, and is the only instrument in the world to give listening practice on a moving source of sound and to furnish a permanent record by automatically and continuously tracing a chart showing pupils' inaccuracies.

They also produced the 'Savage' scanning searchlight,

> ... designed to reveal aircraft at the earliest possible moment, and to illuminate and search in every second an area of sky from fifty to one hundred times greater than the ordinary standard searchlight, and to give a light range greater than the sound range of the most sensitive sound locator.

Early in the Battle of the Atlantic it was found that the sea would interfere with the Radar when trying to detect a surfaced U-boat at night. To solve this problem Squadron Leader Humphrey de Verd Leigh came up with the idea of a powerful searchlight for use by RAF patrols. Jack Savage led in assisting in the trial and development of the Leigh Light (L/L) before Savage and Parsons began its production in mid-1942. The device was designed to fit under a bomber and a modified Wellington proved the ideal aircraft to carry it. The 24-inch searchlight was fitted in a retractable under-turret controlled by a hydraulic motor and ram. By the end of 1944, Coastal Command had

119 Wellingtons equipped with the L/L and it remained in use until the end of the war. A smaller version was produced to fit under the wing of the Catalina or Liberator. The L/L proved so successful it forced the U-boats to take the risk of surfacing in daylight to charge their batteries. Savage and Parsons also made a VHF duplex telephony unit, the 'Savage set', in their works in Kingsbury that incorporated a quench circuit to make the signal undecipherable to someone without the same type of receiver. Jack Savage died in September 1945 only weeks after the final surrender.

Wild-Barfield Electric Furnaces was another company that supplied the aircraft industry. In 1939 they were situated at 4-8 Highwood Avenue in Bushey, but they soon moved to a new location at the Elecfurn Works on Watford Bypass. They made electric furnaces for every form of heat-treatment in the aircraft and general engineering industries and importantly the heated light alloy billets for treating forgings, castings and other fabricated light alloy parts.

In 1927 Scammell Lorries, the successful truck manufacturers in Tolpits Lane, had developed the Pioneer, a high performance 6x4 heavy haulage

Vickers Wellington GR Mark XIV, HF197 '1-D' of RAF Coastal Command 172 Squadron fitted with a Leigh Light undergoing servicing at Lagens in the Azores where an anti-submarine detachment was based between December 1943 and April 1944 (Air Ministry, public domain)

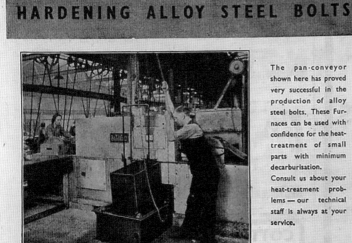

HARDENING ALLOY STEEL BOLTS

CONVEYOR FURNACE

The pan-conveyor shown here has proved very successful in the production of alloy steel bolts. These Furnaces can be used with confidence for the heat-treatment of small parts with minimum decarburisation. Consult us about your heat-treatment problems — our technical staff is always at your service.

The equipment has a rating of 39 kw and operates normally at 850° C. whilst the useful dimensions are 20 inches wide by 2½ inches high. By using a variable gear box incorporated under the Furnace a wide range of speed of travel may be obtained. Other sizes are available giving outputs from 1 cwt. to 4 cwt. per hour.

ELECTRIC WILD BARFIELD FURNACES

WILD-BARFIELD ELECTRIC FURNACES LTD.
ELECFURN WORKS, WATFORD BY-PASS, WATFORD, HERTS
Telephone: WATFORD 6094 (4 lines). *Telegrams:* ELECFURN, WATFORD

M-W.85

Wild-Barfield newspaper advertisement 1943 (public domain)

tractor for cross-country use. By early 1932 they had begun investigating its potential as a tank transporter. After the Pioneer had proved itself on rough roads in the colonies, particularly in the oil and timber industries, a version, the R100, was developed for military use. In 1937 a further variant was produced with a longer chassis to allow for an enlarged cab to take tank crew as passengers. The army duly purchased the R100 equipped with a folding crane and towing gear as a recovery vehicle, and another model, the SV2S, was introduced in 1938. On the outbreak of war, Scammell turned all their efforts to the production of the military specification Pioneers, powered by specially designed diesel engines made by Gardner and Sons of Manchester. The Pioneer, with its own 18-ton semi-trailer and winch, was used as a tank and medium and heavy artillery transport with accommodation for crew, tools, equipment and ammunition and as a recovery vehicle.

During the BEF's retreat to Dunkirk many valuable Pioneer gun transporters were lost in France, either destroyed by the withdrawing troops or captured by the Germans. When the Americans arrived in Britain they found the 20 and 30 ton Pioneers were too tall to take their tanks under British bridges, so they turned to their own Diamond T transporters. It was probably

1939 Scammell R100 HAT Military Lorry, photo Les Chatfield, PDTillmann, 2009

just as well, as Scammell could not keep pace with demand and from late 1943 the R100 heavy artillery tractors had to be supplemented with the Albion CX22S produced in Glasgow. The Pioneers were well respected and the recovery vehicles were said to be superior to their German equivalents. The SV2S breakdown tractors were included in the delivery of British vehicles that found their way to the Eastern Front to bolster the ill-equipped Red Army. The production of Scammell's various models of transporter continued throughout the war, running to over 2,500 vehicles. At the end of the war a number of Pioneers were supplied to the Danish army. The last Pioneer recovery vehicle was not retired from the British army until the 1980s in Belize.

Sun Engraving may have not been such an obvious candidate for being heavily involved in war work but so much activity was diverted from their usual production that the Composing Room was turned completely over to it. The company was required to turn their engineering department to the production of parts for anti-aircraft shells and for bulldozers, excavators, tanks (including gears and wheels for the Matilda) and bearings for Bren gun carriers. They were also involved in a number of top-secret activities

Scammell Pioneer transporter in North Africa loading a Matilda tank, August 1942, Army Film & Photographic Unit (public domain)

including the production of materials for the Manhattan Project – the making of the atomic bomb which ultimately brought an end to the war with Japan. Less devastating but important was the manufacture of 'Mixture', commonly known as 'Windows'; narrow metallic strips of various lengths and frequency responses that acted like small aerials and were used to disable the German radar system. The original aluminium strips proved too light and were replaced by copper and finally tin foil. Their purpose was to conceal the size and direction of an attacking force from the enemy.

Sun's primary role as high-quality printers was still important and in 1943 they were commissioned to produce and print photographs taken from aerial reconnaissance and maps of occupied Europe in preparation for the Allies' D-Day landings in Normandy the following year. Work on what would result in a series of massive loose-leaf volumes collated from the material began in November. Guards were placed at the entrance to partitioned areas within departments and plates and copy were transported between departments in locked containers. The books, later referred to at the Sun as 'the Bible of the invasion', with titles such as *Tactical Targets, Area 4901W (Caen)*, came in three series, code named 'Boxes', 'Cases' and 'Kartons'. Each book in 'Boxes' held 90 to 200 full-page hand-engraved illustrations of targets, which sometimes required over 50 engravings for each photograph. The heaviest book weighed 7.5lbs and contained 360 separate printed items, all hand-collated. 'Cases' covered the strategic bombing of single targets, and 'Kartons' covered targets not dealt with in the first series. 'Pakkets', a fourth series of 46 two-colour books, covered area operations around the rivers Rhine, Ems and Elbe, and the 'Southern Redoubt' on the Danube. From 1942 the Sun's colour facility was used by the Political Intelligence Department to produce propaganda leaflets to be dropped by the RAF. Once the Allied invasion was underway, up to one and a half million of their leaflets were dropped per day over occupied Europe and Germany.

In April 1942 the Sun began publication of an occasional record of their staff's activities serving at home and abroad, *The 'Sun' at War: a Record of Service*. Further issues came out in December 1942 and April and October 1943. It was so successful that it came to the notice of Field Marshal Montgomery who said in a letter to the company written in September 1944, 'I always thought that the Magazine was a very good idea, which other business concerns might well copy.' In common with most industries, Sun Engravers employed a large number of women. Although some worked in the pressroom on traditional Sun items such as *Country Life*, due to censorship restrictions little was revealed concerning their war related work. An item in the October 1943 issue, *'Sun' girls at work*, gave a rare insight as to the 'girls' working on the copper depositing process, a highly toxic method of electrolytical copper plating, a job normally carried out by experienced electroplaters. These skilled workers were in short supply so female replacement volunteers had been recruited, many from the warehouse, to do the increasingly large amount of plating and anodizing work required, possibly for printed circuits. The magazine's final issue, *The 'Sun' at War: A Record of Victory* (October 1945), praised these volunteers who 'brought great energy and ability to a type of work unlike any they had done before'. The issue also carried a list of all the Sun staff drafted into the forces.

Like Sun Engravers, Odhams' presses in North Watford were put to work printing millions of instructional and propaganda leaflets. At the beginning of the war their leaflets were dropped on Germany and again in 1944 to coincide with the D-day landings. In addition, their experience as magazine publishers was turned to producing the magazine *Yank* for the US army, and similar publications for the French, Dutch and Italian liberation forces. Odhams' newly enlarged site was big enough to accommodate facilities for repairing aircraft for the Ministry of Aircraft Production.

Paper was a vital commodity and in short supply, but also a versatile medium. At John Dickinson and Co's Croxley Mill, the company produced special quality paper for maps and board caps. More impressively, Dickinsons were called on to convert their paper mill sites into factories for manufacturing a whole variety of military related products. Containers made from paper were designed to carry munitions and even more ingeniously the paper petrol tanks for long-range fighters and bombers that could be jettisoned after use, enabling them to fly further without refuelling. They also made aircraft fuel pumps, cardboard boxes for gas masks, blackout paper, a variety of munitions and, like Sun Engravers, the special foil dropped to confuse enemy radar. Rationing meant the raw materials for papermaking were difficult to obtain, but despite this Dickinsons' business did not suffer. Although the demand for paper dropped heavily, they had diverted around 80 per cent of their production to requirements for the Ministry of Defence.

John Laing & Co, a company that would go on to be one of the largest construction companies in the country, had its headquarters at Mill Hill. They were a major developer of airfields – they were responsible for RAF Bovingdon – and at their works at Elstree they produced one of the type of temporary and pre-fabricated buildings that were much needed for the rapid construction of airfield sites, the 'Laing' hut, made of light timber and plasterboard sheets. When it was time for D-Day, John Laing were one of the contractors for the construction of the Mulberry Harbour units used for the landings.

Aircraft Production

One of the most important wartime sectors of industry was aircraft production and it was one in which the area was heavily involved. In preparation for war the government developed the Shadow Factory Scheme, a strategy to use existing motorcar manufacturing facilities for aircraft production. Although the heartland of car manufacturing was in the North and the Midlands, there were a number of companies involved in truck and coach building in the London area (Chrysler at Kew, Duple in Hornsey, Express Motor & Bodyworks Ltd in EC1, and Park Royal Coachworks). In 1940, the London manufacturers were formed into a parallel consortium known as the London Aircraft Production Group (LAPG) under the leadership of London Transport in cooperation with the Second Aircraft Group (SAG) administrated by de Havilland. The major activity of the LAPG was the production of Handley Page Halifax bombers for the RAF, as well as ammunition, gun parts, armoured vehicles and spare parts for vehicles. Aircraft production was a high priority industry and large numbers of workers, over half female, were drafted into the LAPG with little experience or training. At its peak the group's 51,000 workers were producing one Halifax bomber per hour, the first delivered in 1941 and the last, named *London Pride*, in April 1945.

The LAPG had 41 factories or sites and 600 sub-contractors, and throughout southwest Hertfordshire small firms became busy supplying components for the industry. London Transport's own works at Chiswick was not capable of dealing with the increased demand so they converted their site near Elstree on land adjacent to the Watford Bypass and today occupied by the Centennial Park industrial estate. The site had been purchased for car sheds for the proposed expansion of the Northern Line to Bushey Heath on which work had already begun. Known as the Aldenham Works, the railway depot was swiftly converted to Halifax production; the planned railway extension never went ahead and was abandoned in 1949. Near to the Aldenham Works, along Elstree Road, aero-engines were tested in a factory that in 1956 was converted into a film studio in the Lismirrane Industrial Park.

Handley Page had their headquarters close by just north of Radlett. In 1928 one of their test pilots had been forced to make a bad weather emergency landing between an unused railway line and Watling Street on a strip of agricultural land. It was a fortuitous event because the company needed room to expand and the following year they moved their production base from Cricklewood Aerodrome to this new site, officially opened by Prince George in July 1930. Initially Radlett aerodrome remained a grass strip where aircraft were assembled from parts made elsewhere. Ten years later it was upgraded to three hard runways and a flight test hangar was built for use in the production of their twin-engine Hampden and four-engine Halifax bombers constructed using components manufactured at several sites in the area. The Hampden took part in the RAF's first raid on Berlin in August 1940. At the peak of production in 1944, between 38 and 42 Halifax bombers were turned out every month.

In January 1940, spacious playing fields known as Mile Field had been purchased by the Ministry of Aircraft Production and leased to the LAPG and SAG. The site was turned into a new airfield known as RAF Leavesden, boasting large purpose-built workshops and hangars and a suitable runway for heavy bombers, perfect for the production and assembly of the Halifax bomber. Here again planes could be assembled and then flight-tested under the supervision of de Havilland. The first Halifax flew from Leavesden on 8 December 1941 and thereafter 710 bombers were assembled there, the last leaving in April 1945. De Havilland began the manufacture of their own Mosquito fighter-bomber at Leavesden soon after; 1,476 Mosquitoes were produced there including 50 Mosquito Torpedo Bombers, 20 per cent of the plane's construction.

De Havilland's own factory at Hatfield, where most Mosquitoes were built (3,326), was put on a war footing from the outset. It was the home of the Tiger Moth, their famous trainer, and the Flying Training School. The Tiger Moth and a number of their other civil aircraft were quickly converted to military use and hundreds of would-be RAF and Commonwealth pilots passed through the Training School, many going on to have illustrious wartime careers. The site carried out a number of other activities, including repair work on Hurricanes, but the facility was most notable for the testing and production of the Mosquito after its initial development at Salisbury

Above and previous page: *The remains of Radlett runway today (Mike Dyer)*

Hall. Innovation at de Havilland did not end with the Mosquito. From 1941 onwards the company's designers began secretly working on prototype jet aeroplanes, a number of which were tested, culminating in the Hornet. This was delivered to the RAF in 1945, but too late to see action. The innovation was not wasted but put to good use after the war when de Havilland turned to civil aviation, producing the first passenger jet airliner, the Comet, in 1962.

Grace's Guide to British Industry list a number of Watford and local companies that supplied parts for the de Havilland Mosquito:

Mosquito prototype W4050 on its maiden flight at Hatfield, 1940 (RAF, public domain)

In Watford

Cox & Co	Plastic radome assemblies
Novo Bax	Machined parts
Watford Electric (WEMCO)	Electrical assemblies

In Herts

Addis Brush, Hertford	Machined components
Brylock Equipment, Letchworth	Machined components
Challis Brothers, Berkhamsted	Machined components
Chater-Lea, Letchworth	Machined components
Education Supplies Assoc, Stevenage	Wings
Hearle Whitley, Letchworth	Machined components
Henderson Safety Tanks, Elstree	Fuel tanks, oil tanks
Hertfordshire Rubber, Letchworth	Rubber components
Jigs (Leavesden)	Machined components
K&C Ironfounders, Letchworth	Metal fittings
Nico, Letchworth	Pressings
AR Parsons, London Colney	Metal fittings
Royal National Lifeboat Inst, Elstree	Tail and rudder fitting

R Sanders, Stevenage   Metal fittings
Vincent-HRD, Stevenage   Manifold pressings
Young & Wilson, Hatfield   Metal fittings

Hatfield was also the permanent base for a number of elite women ferry pilots serving with the Air Transport Auxiliary, who were needed to transfer aircraft from factories to reserve and operational locations. Their most famous pilot was Amy Johnson, the first woman to fly solo from Britain to Australia. She died in disputed circumstances in 1941 when her Airspeed Oxford came down in the Thames in bad weather. Her body was never found. Proving the sceptics wrong, the women ATA pilots performed vital work delivering Spitfires and Hurricanes and in 1942 some graduated to flying heavy bombers. Lettice Curtis, the first woman to fly an Avro Lancaster, flew Halifax bombers from Radlett.

In the early 1930s a field in Elstree was converted into a landing strip for the private planes of members of Aldenham House country club. During the war the airfield was upgraded and a concrete runway put down making it suitable for aircraft manufacture. From 1941 Fairfield Aviation, who employed 1,100 people from the Watford area, used the site for repairs and modification work on a number of aircraft including the Westland Lysander III. The hangars (which still stand) are said to have been built for the modification of Wellington bombers that, when part assembled and without wings, were towed up the Watford Bypass from a factory in Watford to be completed there with further modifications fitted. It is rumoured these modifications included those necessary to carry out the early bouncing bomb trials. Fairfield were working out of three sites in Watford including Odhams. In total 1,809 aircraft were worked on, mainly comprising 473 Wellingtons and 1,217 Lysanders. The site was also used by the Allied Expeditionary Air Forces Communication Squadron, who maintained a detachment of aircraft there during late 1944, the No. 124 Gliding School and the Central Link Trainer School.

Amy Johnson by John Capstack c.1933-5 (public domain)

The BBC at Aldenham

'This is London Calling' was the call sign of the BBC World Service, and the sound of Derek Prentice's familiar voice would have been eagerly anticipated across the globe, particularly in enemy occupied areas. But after October 1940 the statement was strictly untrue;

Broadcasting House had been badly damaged by a bomb and his voice was no longer actually coming from London. The Overseas Service had been sent on a walkabout, initially to Abbey Manor in Evesham and then on to Aldenham House, which for a short while became one of the BBC's three main studio centres for the External Services. The other centres were still in London, at Bush House in the Strand, and from June 1941, at the requisitioned East Block of Peter Robinson's department store at 200 Oxford Street. Once installation work was completed on the spacious 'PR building' in Oxford Street, the Overseas Services from Aldenham and the Radio Newsreel from Abbey Manor were transferred there overnight at the end of May 1942. Aldenham House continued as a switching centre for overseas broadcasts sending out Allied propaganda to the Middle East and Latin America.

Ron Chown, who went on to have a post-war career in the BBC, recalled how as a 16-year-old schoolboy in 1943 he was recruited into the Corporation. One of his ATC officers, who worked for the BBC's recording department, was seeking 'Youth-in Training' recruits (YiTs) and Ron and three of his friends applied. After an interview with the engineer in charge at Aldenham House, Mr Radford, he was taken on, along with a fellow school-leaver and two other YiTs. To get to Aldenham, the recruits were picked up by a green BBC bus from opposite Edgware underground station. Ron was paid £1/7/6d a week plus a 4/6d cost of living bonus; night shifts, during which any spare time was used to make sure that all the plugs on the cords were clean and well polished, were paid extra.

Aldenham transmitted on two networks, 'Pink' and 'Brown'. Brown, the Arabic Service, was the more established and went out early at 4 am. During the night the network switched from about eleven o'clock to a Portuguese language Latin American broadcast mainly for Brazil. Pink was used as the Spanish Latin America network. As well as working at Aldenham, the trainees were sent to the Maida Vale and Evesham studios to learn broadcasting theory. They then took an exam before being posted. Ron's preference was to go back to Aldenham or to stay in London, but he was sent to Bedford as a technical assistant before he was able to return to Aldenham. In the meantime, new networks had been added to the European Services and hours extended on the old ones. It was now 1944 and when the news came of the D-Day landings it was put out on the Overseas Service linked up to the USA network giving Derek Prentice an estimated audience of 100 million.

After the war, in February 1946, members of BBC staff who had been in the services started to return, so Ron, who had been in a reserved occupation, had to take his turn to do national service. As he lived in London close to Hertfordshire he joined the Beds & Herts regiment. Aldenham House stood empty until purchased in 1959 and was occupied by the Haberdashers' Aske's Boys' School in 1961.

The Grove: Project X

Some organizations did not wait to be bombed before moving their staff out of London. The government had advised large undertakings to move from towns and cities that could be targeted and after Italy invaded Albania in April 1939, the London, Midland & Scottish Railway (LMS) bought The Grove to be its headquarters in the event of war. Lineside Estates, a subsidiary of LMS, negotiated the £80,000 purchase of the one-time residence of the Earl of Clarendon from The Equity & Law Life Assurance Company in secret, and the proposed move was known as 'Project X'. Work then began on turning the house into office space with extra accommodation provided in camouflaged huts built, for safety reasons, spread around the estate. By Friday, 1 September, all was ready. The first many of the staff of Britain's largest railway company knew about the move was when they were suddenly given personal printed notices telling them that on Monday they had to make their way from their Euston office to Watford Junction Station. On arrival, transport would be laid on to take them to location 'X'. They were asked to bring their gas masks and food for the day and an unbreakable drinking vessel. Once at The Grove they were required to make their way to the allocated 'Hutment' for their department. As war was declared on the Sunday, the LMS were credited with one of the swiftest moves out of the capital; in one day 3,000 of their employees had been transferred to their new temporary home. It was not quite a seamless manoeuvre as not all the required huts had been completed and many of the staff were happy to find that as a result they only needed to turn up three days a week.

The move was almost like a military operation. Three thousand individuals had been uprooted and suddenly dumped miles from anywhere, with no shops, nowhere to eat, and the nearest pub a mile away. At first conditions were basic – the huts were provided with a number of coke boilers, which could be used for making tea and cooking snacks – but over time improvements were made that turned the site into a self-contained camp. To counter the winter mud, a network of concrete paths was laid and concrete underground air raid shelters built (some of which remain) and used when on occasion some bombs did land on the estate (causing minimal damage). A gentleman's barbers and lady's hairdressers were established in one of the stables with professional hairdressers from London and there was a General Store staffed by members of the Euston Co-operative Society. A large staff canteen was built. Here was served a range of filling non-meat dishes that, making the best of the available ingredients, often consisted of rare vegetables of unknown origin.

The estate's walled garden was turned into a vegetable patch and tomatoes were grown in the Victorian greenhouses, so to complement the frugal diet, some of this produce was available for a price. In addition, on land adjoining the canal, staff members were able to grow their own vegetables on allotments let at a shilling a pole. These allotments were outside the grounds so staff had to be given special permits to enter and leave the grounds outside office hours. To add a bit of colour, the ground around the huts was cultivated and an annual flower show held. Other leisure activities were arranged: 'mixed cricket' was a summer favourite, and when the lake (now filled in) froze for two weeks there was the opportunity for ice-skating. Whether it was work or leisure, horse chestnuts were collected each autumn at the request of the Ministry of Food to supply animal feed.

The work at The Grove was of critical importance. As the main artery for the movement of goods, munitions and service personnel, the railway network had to be kept operational despite being under constant aerial attack. The LMS had 250,000 employees at the outbreak of war and success depended on their teamwork. Staff were required to work long and hard to keep the 'lines behind the lines' open. Their HQ was an integral part of coordinating the system and needed to maintain good communication with the Railway Executive that controlled the four mainline railway companies (LMS, Great Western, Southern and London & North Eastern) and the London Transport system. To this end an efficient telegraph office was installed to maintain direct contact with the Railway Executive, the main railway locations and various government ministries. The Railway Executive's wartime HQ was in the disused Down Street underground station in Mayfair and it was shared in time of need by Churchill and his war cabinet. In the end the enemy never succeeded in bringing the railways to a halt, a tribute to the efforts of the workers of the Home Front.

CHAPTER SEVEN

The Tide Turns

By early 1941 Britain was facing its darkest hour, with the home front bearing the brunt of the hardships; 40,000 civilians killed and 50,000 injured during air raids while U-boat disruption of shipping convoys meant shortages in the shops. Greece, the last mainland European outpost standing against the Axis forces, fell at the end of April leaving Britain and its Empire and Commonwealth allies alone to carry on the fight in the North Atlantic, North Africa and the Mediterranean against the combined strength of Germany, Italy, Russia and their acolytes. But within the year two major events were to change the balance of the war. In June, just as Crete's heroic defence finally crumbled giving the Axis powers virtual mastery of the Mediterranean, Hitler decided to rip up his treaty with Stalin (the Molotov-Ribbentrop Pact, August 1939) and launch Operation Barbarossa, the invasion of the USSR. In the belief that the Russians would be quickly subdued, the road would then be clear for a final all-out attempt on Britain before President Roosevelt might move US policy from merely giving aid to Britain to actively joining the war in Europe as its ally. Overnight, Operation Barbarossa turned Russia from Britain's to Germany's foe and therefore into Britain's friend. The advantages of the new rebalancing appeared to be short-lived when Japan took its eagerly awaited opportunity to seize European and American interests in south-east Asia and the Pacific. On the morning of 7 December 1941 they made their fateful unprovoked attack on the American naval base at Pearl Harbor in Hawaii. Although British and Commonwealth territories were also attacked the greater long-term strategic effect was the forcing of America's hand. Four days later Japan's Axis partners, Germany and Italy, had declared war on America bringing the USA directly into the war in Europe. The stretched British and Commonwealth forces had gained another powerful ally; and the weight of American military might in addition to Russian resistance on the Eastern Front ultimately put the contest in the favour of the Allies.

From 1942 onwards the four powers, the US, Britain, Russia and in the East, China, began planning how to take the war to the enemy. This meant that the Home Front would no longer be a defensive line, and increasingly troops were to be posted abroad. As the threat of a hostile invasion waned, it was replaced by a real 'friendly invasion' from across the Atlantic that would have a profound impact on the locals.

The Americans are coming

The first American servicemen began arriving in Britain in January 1942, armed with a booklet entitled *Instructions for American Servicemen in Britain* giving advice on how to deal with the natives. South West Hertfordshire was soon to become home to a number of US military establishments at various locations from Ashridge to Bushey. After two years of wartime austerity, visitors to the centre of Watford had to accustom themselves to the shock of seeing the High Street suddenly full of smartly dressed American servicemen. Within walking distance from the centre, American troops had been based in a camp in fields off Langley Way near Cassiobury Park. The medical rehabilitation centre at High Elms Manor in Garston became a source of conjecture when a number of pillboxes were erected around it. It was reportedly used for consultation and liaison between the US and British air forces (after the war it reverted to medical use as a National Health Service property for the treatment of elderly patients).

The American Air Force flying the Stars and Stripes at Bushey Hall, 1944 (Bushey Museum)

Helen 'Nellie' Hurndall of Avenue Rise, Bushey, getting in some small arms practice at Bushey Hall (Bushey Museum)

Bushey Hall, also within easy distance of the town centre, became an HQ of the American Air Force (USAAF). The hotel, a training school for officer cadets during the First War, had been requisitioned again in 1942, this time by RAF Fighter Command due to its proximity to their headquarters at Bentley Priory. With America in the war it was soon passed over to the 8th Air Force Fighter Command (part of the American 8th Army), becoming station 341, codename Ajax. The US Bomber Command HQ was reasonably close by at High Wycombe. As there was no airstrip, the main task undertaken

WAACs plotting on data boards (Bushey Museum)

was to coordinate and plot the missions of fighter escorts for bombing raids into enemy territory, but in addition it was the main receiver for intelligence on Axis forces and troop movements. In common with the RAF, many of the administrators and plotters were women, in this case, members of the American Women's Air Corps. Around 10,000 American servicewomen were at some time stationed in the UK during the war. To cope with the extra demands, several buildings had to be erected in the grounds and some of these Nissen huts and concrete structures remain today. The golf course, on which sheep were grazed, offered an opportunity for exercise and relaxation. After an unfortunate sheep was shot during target practice, this activity was discontinued, but General Eisenhower and three companions were said to have played a round on the course.

The largest USAAF base nearby was at Bovingdon Aerodrome. Bovingdon was handed over by the RAF in May 1942 but the first American airmen did not take up residence until August. When the 92nd (Heavy) Bombardment Group took over the tenancy, the airfield became home to one of the most iconic aircraft of the war, the Boeing B-17 or 'Flying Fortress'. Bovingdon was used mainly as an operational training base and by the Air Technical Section who were responsible for testing fighters. This meant a variety of other aircraft types flew from the site. In addition, specialist RAF personnel were seconded to share their expertise and the OSS (forerunner of the CIA) used it as a transportation station. Despite the heavy commitment to training, the 92nd were called on to fly a few combat missions. In September and October they took part in raids over France and Belgium, suffering the first American heavy bomber losses of the war. The high-level close formation daylight raids favoured by the Americans initially proved costly and the Group was assigned the role of a B-17 Combat Crew Replacement Unit (CCRU), training and supplying new recruits to fill gaps in other units. In January 1943, the 92nd, apart from 326th Bomb Squadron, was transferred to RAF Alconbury, near Huntingdon, where it was reformed as an operational combat group, leaving the 326th to form the core of the 11th CCRU. Most bombing combat crews received their introduction here before moving on to their operational bases.

After pressure from the US media, in February 1943 high-altitude training was given to journalists and newsreel cameramen so that they could accompany combat missions over Europe. The eight journalists chosen to undergo this training, known as the 'Writing 69th', included Walter Cronkite ('the Voice of America' from the *United Press*), James Denton Scott (*Yank, the Army Weekly*), Homer Bigart (*New York Herald Tribune*), William Wade (*International News Service*) and Gladwin Hill (*Associated Press*). During an attack on the German submarine pens at Wilhelmshaven there were heavy losses and the aircraft of Andy Rooney (*Stars and Stripes*) was damaged by flak and Robert Post (*New York Times*) was killed when his B-24 exploded.

Huts at USAAF Bushey Hall c. 1944 (Bushey Museum)

A British reporter was also killed on a mission over Kiel from Bassingbourn airfield. After these losses it was decided to terminate the scheme.

Bovingdon became a major staging post for aircraft coming from and returning to the States and its closeness to command HQs and London meant that a number of 'top brass' passed through. It was the base of the 'A' Flight of Headquarters Squadron and the Supreme Allied Commander, General Dwight Eisenhower, had his personal B-17 housed in Hangar 1 on the base. Several film stars were assigned at one time or another to the base, including Clark Gable, who ran a motion picture unit while serving in B-17s as an observer-gunner, James Stewart, who led combat missions and had a number of staff jobs, rising to the rank of colonel, and William Holden who made training films. Other famous wartime visitors were Bob Hope, Frances Langford, Eleanor Roosevelt (whose son Elliot was a lieutenant colonel serving there) and Glen Miller. In June 1943 the most famous B-17, *Memphis Belle*, having completed twenty-five combat missions, was flown back home from Bovingdon to undertake a tour to raise war bonds. The plane became the subject of two films, a 1944 documentary *Memphis Belle, the study of a Flying Fortress* directed by William Wyler and the 1990 drama *Memphis Belle* directed by Michael Caton-Jones.

In September 1944, the CCRU was disbanded and Bovingdon became the base for the Air Transport Service ferrying troops and supplies to France, Italy and eventually Germany. Once victory had been secured, it became a major departure point for thousands of Americans returning home. They were the lucky ones; 154 aircraft took off from Bovingdon never to return.

An airfield in a small place like Bovingdon was bound to have a tremendous effect on the locality. Up until then it had been largely a farming community of around a thousand souls. Suddenly a village that had already taken in evacuees and refugees had to cope with the presence of 2,000 Americans. Soon the local pubs were swamped with 'Yanks' many of whom came from 'dry' areas of the United States and had never tasted alcohol before. Although meals were served on camps, not all camps were fully residential. A number of service personnel and officers had to be billeted amongst the locals, those from Bovingdon being put up in and around Hemel Hempstead. Families that took in American servicemen were reimbursed around £2 2s for a room and bed under the lend-lease agreement between the US and the UK. On the whole the GIs, as they were commonly known, proved courteous and generous guests and many warm ties were formed with their hosts. If a GI had a camera, photographs were taken and exchanged, and treasured, as photographic film was unavailable at the time in Britain. With the host nation in its third year of wartime austerity the Americans' access to luxuries and exotic items (fruit, cookies, Hershey bars, chewing gum, nylon stockings, Lucky Strike cigarettes, Jack Daniels) from their stores could make them popular and their generosity with goodies went down well with young children. A common occurrence was for kids on seeing an American soldier

The crew of the Memphis Belle *on completion of twenty-five missions and flying home from Bovingdon (public domain)*

to ask, 'Yank, got any gum?' Less innocently, it was commonly assumed that if a girl possessed that rarest of commodities, nylon stockings, she had paid intimately for them and was the subject of moral indignation for years after. Added to this the GIs were comparatively well paid, receiving £3 10s (£3.50) per week to their British counterpart's 17 shillings and sixpence (87½p). If not handled sensitively, their advantages combined with a natural American forwardness were often interpreted as cocky.

As the GIs did not possess civilian clothes, they would always be seen in uniform in town, a sight that impressed many of the local girls as they showed off their knowledge of the latest dance crazes, such as the Jitterbug, at the regular dances at Watford Town Hall. That some of the girls were prepared to fall for the visitors is borne out by the establishment of 'prophylactic stations' in Hemel Hempstead and Chesham, which after protest from the health authorities were renamed more discretely as 'first aid stations'. For some local women, relations with the GIs may have been merely a cynical transaction and there was reportedly a 'house of ill-repute' in Bovingdon for

Officers' Post Exchange Store at Bushey Hall with goodies on display including Milky Ways, cigars and alcohol (Bushey Museum)

the Americans. The perceived attitude of the GIs that the local girls were fair game led to jealousy and resentment, and the occasional bit of trouble at the local dances necessitated the military police being on hand. The GIs were not the only foreign military, there were Commonwealth troops and fighters from occupied Europe, such as the Poles and the French, but they were the most numerous and ostentatious. On one occasion matters turned ugly in the Lower High Street when a GI struck a girl. Some local onlookers then pitched in, joined by a number of Canadian soldiers. A general melée ensued during which the American military police who had appeared on the scene resorted to firing shots at the threatening crowd and in the aftermath seven of the participants had to be taken to hospital with stab wounds.

Many Americans were unfamiliar with British ways and there were tensions caused by cultural misunderstandings. As a number of the GIs came from the Southern States where various degrees of official and unofficial racial segregation were in force, they were unaccustomed to mixing with their black comrades. When the black and white GIs found themselves frequenting the same pubs this could cause a problem and when a fuss was made at a dance at the Town Hall an unofficial colour bar was introduced. Not all Watford residents were so compliant when it came to segregation. Despite their aversion to warm beer the pubs were popular with the GIs, leading to the accusation they were drinking the places dry. One of their haunts was the Wellington Arms in Watford run by Harry Kent, the retired Watford FC manager. When American officers asked him not to serve black American troops, he retorted it was his pub and he would serve whomsoever he wanted. For the Americans who found these local delights wanting there was alternative entertainment to be had at base. The US (United Services) Camp Tours organised the visits of celebrities to entertain the troops. Merle Oberon and Al Jolson came to Watford and Bob Hope and his troupe, which included Francis Langford and Jerry Colonna, performed at Bushey Hall. Glen Miller and his orchestra, who held concerts at Bovingdon, were rumoured to have played there but the concert actually took place at Bentley Priory. Miller and his band had their base in Bedford.

An article by Randolph Woolley on serving American airmen includes the recollections of Marshal Stelzriede, who was stationed at Bovingdon in 1943. Stelzriede gives us an intriguing American viewpoint of life in wartime Hertfordshire. As well as cycling around the countryside to take in its quaint delights, he recalled there were ample opportunities for social life:

> There were dances (mainly the old-fashioned type) on several evenings of each week in the town hall at nearby Watford, and crewmen were allowed liberal off-base passes. There were also frequent forays to the restaurants in town. In the throes of wartime rationing, food in the restaurants was by no means of the very best quality. Most common in the fast-food type

*of restaurants were fish and chips, and brawn and chips. Brawn was
similar to American blood sausage, and what they called 'chips' were
like our French fries. A restaurant on High Street featured small, but very
good, steaks which the owners preferred to sell to Americans, because
the higher-paid Yanks tipped better than service men of other countries.*

If the portions appeared meagre, the Ministry of Food were happy to announce
that the nations diet was healthier and better than it had been pre-war, despite
an increase in rationing. Stelzriede's musings on British eating habits show
some bemusement with our obsession with tea-breaks:

*We were also introduced to tea and crumpets at about that time. British
workers on the air base had tea at 8:30 and 10:00, lunch at 12:00, tea
again at 1:30 and 4:00, and dinner at 6:00 PM. It was irreverently
claimed that Royal Air Force pilots would pull up alongside a cloud to
have their tea at the appropriate time.*

For those who wanted brighter lights than Watford could offer, London's
Piccadilly was not far away, and it was eagerly taken advantage of.

The Americans were well aware of the need to be on good terms with the
locals. They were willing to lend a hand getting in the harvest in the nearby
farms and Father Christmas made appearances at children's Christmas dinners
at Bushey Hall or at Bovingdon, where he gave presents to orphans. On the
whole the Americans got on well with their hosts; they had to, because there
was no opportunity for home leave. Many stayed for the duration of the war,
and after so many years there were the inevitable, although not encouraged,
romances. The base chapel at Bushey Hall witnessed a number of marriages
between local girls and American servicemen.

On the front foot

Even though fires could be still observed from raids on London, a new
optimism was in the air. The sound of bombers rumbling overhead was no
longer necessarily a threat and it lifted the spirits of those on the ground
as they realised the fight was being taken to the enemy. But there were new
dangers, this time not from bombs or planes brought down in dogfights
overhead, but from the increase in the Allied bomber missions. In September
1941 a Whitley bomber came down just off Finch Lane, Bushey, where it
exploded on landing. On 22 August 1943, a Lancaster bomber (I L7575 UG-
Q) from 1654 Heavy Conversion Unit, an RAF training unit, under the
command of F/O Eric Williams took off from Wigsley. It was on a simulated
night bombing attack known as Command Bullseye. Just after 8 pm, debris
rained from the skies over Warren House Farm at Colney Heath. The cause

USAAF hut at Bushey Hall today (Mike Dyer)

was thought to have been very severe turbulence and, possibly, icing on the outer wings and tail of the aircraft leading to structural failure. All of the crew of seven, which included two Australians, were killed.

Some planes were forced to make emergency landings in the fields round about. A Lancaster limping towards Bovingdon hit trees near Chenies Manor and was forced to make an emergency landing in nearby fields. Some were not so lucky. The Bovingdon area saw a number of crashes as damaged aircraft tried to land. An American Lockheed P-38 fighter crashed in a field next to Whippendell Hall in Chipperfield. When returning from a raid many aircraft would be badly shot up and one crew returning to base at Bovingdon was forced to bail out before reaching the tarmac, leaving the B-17 to crash some miles further on. Locals believed a stricken B-17 that crashed in Brickett Wood Common had done so to avoid hitting houses nearby. On another occasion in 1944 the crew of a shot-up Liberator, *Flexible Flier*, bailed out over Suffolk expecting the plane to crash into the North Sea, instead it landed just behind some houses in Sarratt! Mrs Farnham of Deadman's Ash is said to have returned to her scullery after hearing a crash to find a Liberator engine lying there. A Canadian bomber that came down in Chorleywood killing the pilot was said to have been hit by friendly fire around Slough. In Watford a Flying Fortress that had hit power lines in a fog crashed in Chequers Lane and a reconnaissance Spitfire ended up in Chilcott Road. An RAF Liberator crashed in a field next to Garston Rehabilitation Centre killing the crew and on the night of the attack on Arnhem a glider made a good landing by the A41, but unfortunately the Albemarle towing plane crashed into the side of Wall Hall killing the crew.

Witnesses on the ground would watch in helpless horror as such incidents happened and thank their lucky stars when they were not involved in the fallout. Living near an airfield meant the likelihood of seeing crashes and Bovingdon and the area round about was particularly prone to incidents. On a night training mission in October, a B-17 out from Bovingdon lost its bearings, hit a hill and came down in a field near Cow Roast lock, Berkhamsted, killing the pilot. The rest of the crew survived. Another well-remembered collision happened over Bovingdon in March 1943 when a circling B17's port wing sliced off the complete tail unit of a Douglas Dakota as it was taking off. At such low level there was no time for the crews to bail out. The Dakota came straight down, and the B17 was only able to fly on for a moment before stalling and coming down in a vertical dive. They crashed two to three hundred yards apart in Whitedell Farm, Belsize, just missing the house. Taking off was a risky business. A B-17 on a weather reconnaissance flight crashed on take-off from the airfield on 9 December 1943, killing the pilot and the crew including two RAF personnel. The American's favoured method of flying Flying Fortresses in close formation while on daylight raids became a common sight, but on occasion the planes would get too close, as when two bombers collided over Letchworth. A mid-air collision is thought to have brought down a B-24 Liberator on a bombing mission. With a payload of bombs on board the crew gave up their lives by staying on board to ensure the plane crashed in fields rather than into a built up area around Cheshunt.

By 1944 Germany was on the retreat in Italy and the Eastern Front and Allied Command finally decided now was the time to strike back at the heart of Nazi-occupied Europe by launching an invasion on French soil. Troop numbers were built up and in the fields of Hertfordshire undercover of trees and hedgerows, military vehicles of all descriptions would be hidden under camouflage. Suddenly, they were all gone. The peculiar large blocks that were hidden at what is now the site of the Hartspring Leisure Centre in Bushey had disappeared to make up the Mulberry Harbours used in the D-Day landings. Residents remember the feeling of euphoria as they were awoken by the continuous roar of aircraft early in the morning of 6 June, looking up to see the sky filled with transport planes and gliders heading for the French coast and realizing that the invasion was underway. The artillery of the St Albans Battery 286th Field Regiment and 86th Field Regiment of the Hertfordshire Yeomanry were landed in France and in the ensuing battles during which they encountered severe resistance and suffered many casualties troop commander Captain Stephen Denys Perry from Bedford won the MC and infantryman Jim Mitchell from Abbots Langley won the MM.

After D-Day there was a dramatic reduction in troop numbers. In June 1944 there were one and a half million GIs in Britain; by the end of Operation Overlord (the Allied invasion) in August the number was reduced to 700,000. The threat of invasion was officially declared over. The few remaining local invasion committees that had been set up to coordinate behaviour under occupation, like the one at Bovingdon, were finally disbanded and the signposts were returned to their normal orientation.

Hitler's last gamble – the Flying Bomb

From 1941 through to 1944, German Command never completely abandoned conventional bombing. In June 1942, Home Farm, Aldenham Park, was seriously damaged by an HE bomb, and there were sixty-four alerts in 1943 when the greatest danger came from unexploded anti-aircraft shells falling to ground. The Germans attempted another last ditch 'baby Blitz' (as the British press dubbed it) in January 1944, during which houses were damaged in Abbots Road, Abbots Langley, a large blast rocked King's Langley and 250 incendiaries fell near Aldenham and Radlett. Croxley Green and Rickmansworth were hit by parachute bombs causing extensive damage and in March it was the turn of Carpenders Park Estate where a flat above a shop was set on fire. But after D-Day, their belief in their ability to change the course of the war with these tactics faded, and by then Hitler had decided to put his faith in Germany's new wonder weapon, the 'Flying Bomb' or V1.

'D Day planes going over June 1944'. Troop-carrying gliders being towed over Bushey Hall (Bushey Museum)

The V1s were nicknamed 'doodlebugs' because of the pulse of their engines. When the engine cut out, the unsettling silence that followed meant the bomb was about to descend, and this combined with the random nature of the attacks made them particularly terrifying. The main target of the 9,500 V1 rockets launched was London, but due to their ineffective guidance system and the efforts of British agents like ZigZag and Tate, most of them either undershot or overshot, which was not good news for areas surrounding the capital. The first V1 to strike locally hit Mill End just before midnight on 15 June 1944. It damaged 309 houses and caused between 14 and 17 casualties, none fatal. V1s reached as far as Hemel Hempstead and Berkhamsted. Thankfully many of the doodlebugs, although terrifying, ended up landing fairly harmlessly in the fields; two V1s landed near Chipperfield, one in Scatterdells Woods, the other hit houses in Whippendell Hill, luckily only causing a few minor injuries. A house was damaged and a cow killed in Radlett and when a V1 landed near Moat Field in Bushey causing damage to 610 houses, including Reveley Cottages almshouses, amazingly only six people and a goat received minor injuries.

If most of the attacks were relatively harmless, it was however a V1 that caused the greatest loss of life in a single strike in Watford. In the early hours

V1 rocket explodes on the Moatfield, Bushey, in the background as WAACs at Bushey Hall parade for a Purple Heart medal ceremony, c1330 hrs on 28 July 1944 (Bushey Museum)

of Sunday, 30 July, a V1 landed in the densely packed terraced streets near the junction of Sandringham Road and Parkgate Road, causing a massive explosion and the deaths of 37 people, including 3 children; 64 people were injured. Numbers vary, but around 50 houses were totally destroyed, 500 other houses were damaged, of which around half were seriously damaged, 100 shops in St Albans Road lost their windows and 2,400 houses sustained minor damage. The reason for so much damage was in part the densely occupied location where the bomb fell, combined with its typical low trajectory that meant a shallow angle of approach and that it may have caught fire before impact. It is alleged that a party attended by American troops was taking place – two GIs are said to have been killed in the blast – and this accounted for a number of the dead. Several of the fatalities were evacuees who had come from London to escape the bombing.

Immediately the hunt for survivors began. The roads were sealed off and a Mobile Listening Squad was called in to detect survivors buried under the rubble. An enquiry centre and temporary mortuary was established at W.H. Lavers timber yard on the corner of Windsor Road and St Albans Road. Parkgate School, which despite being damaged, became a rest centre, and Civil Defence units from Abbots Langley, Rickmansworth, Bushey, Aldenham and Radlett came to assist. In the confusion a number of bodies were misidentified and tally of the dead proved to be overestimated at the time. Immediately after the bomb fell it was assumed that 40 people had died (as recorded on a plaque in North Watford Cemetery); after the war the number was changed to 37 confirmed deaths. Amongst the dead were two pupils, three ex-pupils and nine parents of children from Parkgate School. There were some extraordinary escapes. Doris Ephitite, who was visiting her daughter at 101 Sandringham Road, got up when the siren sounded and then returned to bed next to her husband. After the blast she was extricated alive from the rubble and taken to the school rest centre. Her husband, daughter and granddaughter were killed. Even though the blast was heard for miles around, Jean Abbot in Maude Crescent slept right through it even though the ceiling had collapsed on top of her. Amazingly she was unharmed.

By the Tuesday the homeless who had been put up at the school were billeted elsewhere, and the school playground became a centre for rebuilding operations. Parkgate School staff and the WVS used the infants department as a feeding centre for the workmen, Home Guard and police officers on duty in the area, continuing into the school holidays. In the aftermath, their dedication earned them the thanks of the County and Borough Councils; Dr T.T.B. Wood of North Western Avenue Surgery received the MBE for his unstinting and courageous medical assistance and Fireman Stanley Victor Clark was awarded a BEM for his rescue efforts. Twelve of the victims were buried in a communal grave in North Watford Cemetery and a special service held in honour of the dead at Christ Church.

In the anecdotes surrounding Bushey Hall two further GIs were reported killed by a V2 rocket, the upgraded version of the V1. This may have been the one that landed in Princes Street in Watford that destroyed five houses. One of the GIs was a character known as Spider who had a bit of a reputation as a drinker and for being involved in scrapes. Spider, who was accompanying his sergeant to collect supplies from an army storage depot, had been left behind to look after their Jeep. As the sergeant entered the building the rocket struck. The building and the Jeep were destroyed. It was assumed that both had been killed and next day a memorial service was held for the two fallen comrades on the Golf Course at Bushey Hall. At a discrete distance the alive but dishevelled figure of Spider could have been spotted looking on. He had left his post at the Jeep and gone on a bender at the nearest pub, only to recover his wits the next day completely unaware of events. Having caught the bus back to base he had been just in time to witness his own memorial. Needless to say, this did not go down well with the powers that be and he was charged with going AWOL and disgracing the uniform.

A few other V2s got through. The paddock of an Ovaltine farm in Abbots Langley was hit by a rocket causing some damage and loss of life and another killed twenty-three people in Park Avenue, Potters Bar. The rocket attacks briefly led to another small evacuation of children and families from London, but the danger was short lived and life was beginning to get back to normal. By the autumn of 1944, blackout restrictions were partially lifted, and in November the Home Guard was stood down. The mild Christmas of 1944 became a time of relative plenty with extra rations of sweets, sugar, margarine and meats. The last sirens were heard the following March and the blackout fully terminated in April. On 8 May, the German military capitulated.

CHAPTER EIGHT

The Human Cost

The war's impact on people's lives ranged from major tragedy to minor inconvenience – some dodgy dealers and black-marketeers even managing to turn a profit. Alongside lives lost, there were families split and homes ruined. In Hertfordshire as a whole 256 people were killed and 1,141 injured by bombing with a large proportion of the casualties being in the Watford area. While Watford took the brunt of the bombing, the villages around suffered more bomb attacks than their strategic significance warranted.

Bomb dropped by district

	HE	Incendiary	Parachute Mine	V1	V2
Berkhamsted	116	138	2	3	
Hemel Hempstead	236	329		3	
Rickmansworth	69	46	6	1	
St Albans	41	8			
Watford	444	2,120		7	1

Bombs dropped on villages

	HE	Incendiary	Parachute Mine	V1	V2
Abbots Langley	76	10			
Aldenham and Radlett	96	247			
Bovingdon	14	15			
Bushey	91	900	2		
Chipperfield				2	
Chorleywood	36	11			
Flaunden	8	24			
Kings Langley	48(?)	12(?)			
Oxhey	71	627			
Sarratt	25	75			

Air Raid Casualties

	Deaths	Serious Injury	Slight Injury
Watford Urban & Rural District	71	52	101
Hemel Hempstead Urban & Rural District	9	3	48
Bushey	2		18
Rickmansworth	8	11	43
St Albans	7	5	18
Berkhamsted Urban & Rural District	1	5	1
Chorleywood			2

In total, Hertfordshire was hit by 4,421 high explosives, 30,500 incendiary devices, 106 V1s and 46 V2s. Because of the Sandringham Road tragedy, the Borough of Watford sustained the most fatalities in the region. After the war (in August 1950), a memorial was erected in North Watford Cemetery

Military funeral, possibly of RAF pilot, Flying Officer L.H. Leader who died in March 1940, with Guard of Honour outside St Peter's Church, Bushey Heath (Bushey Museum)

dedicated to all the victims of the V1 rocket but it lists only the names of the twelve who are buried in the cemetery.

In addition many families had to deal with the loss of loved ones serving in the forces. For parents with children serving in the forces part of life would be the worry for their welfare. Parents of missing local boys serving in the Bedfordshire and Hertfordshire Regiment would not know if they were dead or incarcerated in Japanese PoW camps, similarly if they were fighting in North Africa, Italy or France with the Hertfordshire Regiment or Hertfordshire Yeomanry. And as local war memorials show, men and women from the region gave their lives in a number of regiments, in the RAF and Royal Navy, and other services. There was no counselling at the time to deal with the trauma of war, loss of life and injury. Psychological treatments were in their infancy, and people had to come to terms with the situations as best they could. For the wounded like Tom Culverhouse from Watford who was badly wounded in the D-Day landings this meant twenty months in hospital and a lifetime walking with a stick. And as he recalled for the *Watford Observer*, serious injury could mean abandonment by wives and girlfriends for whom sharing a life with a handicapped partner was too much. He was lucky and his marriage endured, but like many veterans the physical and mental scars would remain even when the war had become a memory. Inevitably, the war stretched the resources of health and social care within the community. Normal illness, disease and medical emergencies still continued, but had to be dealt with in addition to the needs of those injured as a result of enemy action. Wartime deprivations increased hardship and stress-related illness, and although most remained stoical, by as early as 1940 the number of suicides had shown an increase. With the hospitals fully stretched, patients suffering from broken limbs might find themselves in a ward full of wounded soldiers, and servicemen wearing blue (a sign they had been injured) would become a common sight on local streets.

Among the preparations the government had taken in anticipation of war was the expansion of hospital facilities around London with huts staffed by Emergency Medical Services (EMS) personnel. In the event, these facilities would provide care for both civilians and servicemen. The country was divided into sectors with both voluntary and local authority hospitals being requisitioned by the EMS. Central London hospitals were to be used as clearing stations and most of their staff and patients were to be transferred out of the capital. University College Hospital (UCH) was in Sector IV covering north-west London and the surrounding district, which meant locations in the Watford area would act as external departments. As early as 3 September 1939, UCH was empty and its patients and staff relocated. As in the First World War there was need for auxiliary hospitals to deal with the pressure on resources, but due to the changes in military tactics that led to less casualties than expected, in the event fewer country houses were taken over as hospitals than previously. Still, the Marquis of Salisbury once again offered Hatfield House as a military Hospital and Broquet Hall became a maternity hospital.

Other famous London institutions were relocated to the region's hospitals. By 1938 the Ministry of Health had already made a compulsory purchase of land in Northwood adjacent to Mount Vernon Hospital to deal with war casualties. Mount Vernon was then a major cancer hospital and it became one of the four sites for the safe storage of radium. As an advance base for Middlesex Hospital it took in patients evacuated from there and, although an EMS hospital, continued with its civilian care, dealing with outbreaks of typhoid in 1943 and smallpox in 1944. Initially 333 of its 979 beds were given over to the wounded. To cater for the extra demand, the grounds were used for temporary accommodation, so that while commissioned officers continued to receive treatment in the wards, other ranks were placed in huts. By 1943 the number of beds had increased to 1,016 of which 946 were designated EMS. The hospital took in wounded French servicemen and German PoWs, which meant keeping them apart. After the war, Mount Vernon continued as a general hospital, but the war years had taken their toll on staff numbers and the hospital was required to take recruits from Lithuania, Belgium and Hungary registered as Displaced Persons (DPs) to fill the vacancies; by 1946 half the staff were foreign.

The first influx of 230 service patients to arrive at Hill End hospital in St Albans in its capacity as part of the EMS came in October 1939. They were mainly chronically ill soldiers who had been accepted into the army in the first rush of mobilization. Hill End Hospital for Mental and Nervous Diseases (the old Hertfordshire County Asylum), with around a thousand beds, became an advance hospital for St Bartholomew's Hospital, requiring its mental patients to be transferred to other hospitals. Most of St Bart's departments were moved from central London and between 1939 and 1947 most of its surgical operations were carried out at Hill End. As a previous mental hospital it lacked surgical facilities and a major refit was required. When the advance party of 5 sisters and 18 nurses arrived they found as well as the beds, 1,000 government-issue stone hot water bottles but little else to nurse the sick. Gas pipes had to be laid and sterilization units and operating theatres created.

In the early months Hill End was still able to deal with civilian patients but then came the calamity of Dunkirk. During May and June 1940, the first major crisis of the war struck the hospitals, and despite the efforts in preparation, at this point numerous schools and private houses were transformed into 'auxiliary hospitals' under the supervision of the Red Cross or St John's Ambulance with doctors provided by the EMS. Hill End was fortunate in having its own railway connection to St Albans City Station and was able to receive 600 wounded from Dunkirk in one week, 321 casualties arriving in one convoy alone. The hospital was now at full capacity with less serious cases put in the grounds. Luckily the weather kept fine. During the Blitz the hospital dealt mainly with air-raid casualties and sick civilians. To convalesce patients from St Albans were sent to the emergency hospital at Ashridge House staffed by Red Cross personnel. As is often the case, the necessities of treating war casualties hastened improvements in medical practice and Barts became a leader in plastic surgery and neurosurgery and by 1944 Hill End was one of the four leading centres for the investigation into penicillin.

Watford Junction was the natural dropping-off point for the wounded to be taken by ambulance to hospitals in and around Watford. Ambulances with the wounded from Dunkirk could be seen making their way to the 'Annexe' of Leavesden Mental Hospital run by the London County Council in Asylum Road. Formerly the St Pancras Industrial School for orphans and vagrant children and then Leavesden Residential School, it had been taken over by the hospital in 1932 to care for senile patients who required little medical treatment. Once requisitioned by the EMS and under UCH control, casualties initially treated in London were moved to the Annexe. To increase capacity, in 1942, 800 additional beds were provided in huts built in the grounds and the following year the LCC (London County Council) were required to hand the Annexe over to the Canadian government as No. 23 Canadian General Hospital, a military hospital for wounded Canadian soldiers. Towards the end of the war it became a Khaki University, part of an educational institution run by the Canadian government for their troops in camps in Britain and France.

Leavesden hospital and Shenley hospital were two other psychiatric hospitals turned over to military use. Shenley, which was only fairly recently built, had half its 2,000 beds given to wounded service personnel and civilians, including wounded prisoners of war. Leavesden Mental Hospital, the old Leavesden Asylum, had seen service in the first war and in a repeat it again suffered staff shortages caused by the enlistment of nurses. With a capacity of 2,209 beds it had been taken over by London County Council in 1930. The LCC designated it to deal solely with mentally handicapped patients, but retained its TB wards. When the Annexe was handed over to the Canadian government, the patients there were transferred back to Leavesden Hospital, with the added complication that children evacuated from the Fountain Hospital in Tooting also had to be found accommodation. This caused severe overcrowding and even the chapel had to be pressed into use as a ward. Again, in 1944, patients were temporarily taken in from St Bernard's Hospital in Hanwell after it suffered bomb damage.

Once the Americans joined the war in 1943, they required their own military hospital and they occupied North Mymms House near Colney Heath. It briefly became the home of the US Army's 1st Surgical Auxiliary Group before becoming the 1st General Hospital. The 7th General Hospital took over in 1944 until the end of the war when the hospital became a demob camp for the ATS and other women's forces. The house went on to be used for film production, notably *Odette* (1950) with Trevor Howard and Anna Neagle, before Hatfield Rural District Council took over the wooden huts on the site to house eighty families. Nearby in North Mymms Park, the home of Major and Mrs Burns had been turned into an Auxiliary Hospital during 1940 by the Joint War Organisation, a combination of the British Red Cross and the Order of St John of Jerusalem. It had room for sixty-six patients drawn from the three services and victims of air raids. Mrs Burns, as commandant, and her three matrons, assisted by Red Cross and Order of St John nurses, tended to 4,497 patients over five years.

The large garage of John Pierpont Morgan Junior's house at Wall Hall had been converted into a Voluntary Aid Hospital Detachment (VAD) hospital during the First World War. When history repeated itself, he set up a Red Cross Hospital at Church farm, a model farm on his estate. Although Wall Hall House had been closed down in 1940 the estate land was still farmed. In contrast to the usual practice of housing officers in higher-class accommodation to the men, the site was used as a convalescent home for all ranks under the supervision of Mr Holland-Hibbert, Viscount Knutsford, who had overseen the VAD hospital during the First World War. Holland-Hibbert lived at his family seat, Munden House, another stately home nearby that was being used as a rest house for Civil Defence workers. The recuperating soldiers were encouraged to partake in various forms of rehabilitation therapy and became a regular sight walking through Aldenham village.

In Watford town itself, the pupils of Reed's School (the London Orphan Asylum) had been evacuated and the buildings requisitioned by the Ministry of Works as a military hospital which took in German PoWs. The newly expanded Watford and District Peace Memorial Hospital came under the control of UCH, its 206 beds supplemented with 104 EMS beds, and in 1941 UCH established outpatients and casualty departments in one of the wards. Shrodells in Vicarage Road became an advance base for both UCH and Charing Cross Hospital and its 578 beds were increased by a further 198. Watford and District Isolation Hospital in Tolpits Lane, extended in 1934 to take 100 beds, was used in 1944 to accommodate Canadian soldiers from the Italian front suffering from diphtheria as a result of wound infection incurred during the Battle of Anzio. In anticipation of air-raid casualties Stanborough Hydrotherapeutic Sanatorium in Stanborough Park, Garston, where the American poet Ezra Pound had once been admitted in 1926 for treatment for mental instability, also came under UCH control. To deal with the likelihood of trauma being suffered by victims of bombing, a neurosis centre was set up with two psychiatric specialists from the Tavistock Clinic. At one point in 1939, when there were only 3 neurotic patients being looked after by the 3 doctors and 35 nurses plus ancillary personnel, one of the patients still managed to escape. The work of the Tavistock clinicians continued in a new vein towards the end of the war when Hatfield House was taken over as a Civil Resettlement Unit and they were transferred there to psychologically assess returning prisoners of war. The task of rebuilding lives had begun.

CHAPTER NINE

Victory

The Allies had to fight all the way to Berlin, and it was only after Hitler's suicide that the Germans conceded defeat. After so much anticipation, when the surrender finally came the outburst of joy after such a hard-won victory was spontaneous and uncontrolled. So much so that people began celebrating the day before the official surrender on Tuesday the 8th of May 1945. The surrender was marked by a public holiday, VE (Victory in Europe) Day, and as church bells rang out for peace crowds gathered and street parties and entertainments were hastily organised. The euphoria was such that the rejoicing went on for two days. Watford Council had thoughtfully invested £50 for flags for the anticipated celebrations and perhaps partly as a result the *Watford Observer* was able to report, 'Watford High-street was a mass of red, white and blue.' Churches flew the Union Jack and on Cawdell's store the national flag was joined by the Stars and Stripes and the Hammer and Sickle. There were 'parades, fun and frolics in parks and on village greens, bonfires (organised and unorganised), street teas for children, fireworks, and all sorts of improvised festivities'. Over 10,000 people turned up to Cassiobury Park to join in the singing and dancing, but unfortunately the scheduled firework display had to be cancelled following a directive from the Home Secretary; it was held the next Wednesday. The unbridled joy of the people could not be controlled. Bonfires were lit with whatever was at hand along the High Street and in Water Lane (arousing the disapproval of the Fire Brigade), people were thrown into the pond or jumped in and there was a near riot on the roundabout outside the Town Hall. Despite the beer shortage somehow the drink flowed. Alan Orchard, a rather intimidated 12-year-old witness, remembered the tall lampposts in the centre of the roundabout being climbed while US military police tried to encourage their men to keep the peace with the aid of their batons. In Aldenham the spectacle of the bonfire had been dangerously augmented with some unexploded incendiaries, and when a large bonfire was built in Fernway in Garston, the more sober residents had the good sense to organise a fire drill just in case.

The war was not in fact over. The Allies were still involved in a dogged war of attrition in the Far East. It would be another three months before Japan surrendered on 14 August, and the formal surrender that brought the Second World War to a conclusion was not made until the 2 September. A two-day public holiday was declared to celebrate VJ Day and once more the crowds

Girl Guide laying a wreath at Bushey Civic War Memorial on Armistice Day 1945
(Bushey Museum)

VE Day celebration in front of the Lotts' factory in Vale Road, Bushey (Bushey Museum)

gathered. Although the public mood was generally one of relief that this was really the end, there were still over five million men and women serving in the British armed services overseas. Demobilization had begun after VE Day but it was to take over a year for some troops to return. For others there would be no return and the long process of rebuilding lives and the country would begin. The dust had hardly settled on the VE day celebrations when in July a general election was held and the Labour party won by a landslide. Watford, which included Bushey, Chorleywood and Rickmansworth, elected the Labour candidate Major John Freeman as its MP and he served the constituency for the next ten years. The more rural Hemel Hempstead in contrast returned their sitting Conservative MP, Viscountess Frances Davidson, who was the only female Tory MP during the parliament.

During the final years of the war, politicians were fully aware that the rebuilding of the peace was going to be a tough task and the planning had already begun. The new government under Clement Attlee began a programme of ambitious reforms that would lead to the nationalisation of utilities and the railways, the founding of the National Health Service and the Welfare State. Unfortunately the peace did not bring an end to wartime austerity and rationing continued; in fact some rationing was increased. The end to rationing was

Land army girls at the VE Day Parade in Broxbourne High Street (Bushey Museum)

VJ Day party in Haydon Road and Cross Street, Oxhey (Bushey Museum)

staggered: bread in 1948, clothes in 1949, petrol in 1950, confectionery and sugar in 1953 and meat and all other food rationing in 1954.

Aftermath

As the new names were added to the war memorials that had been erected to commemorate the dead of the 'war to end all wars' in towns and on village greens or in schools or work places, like the one in the garden at Apsley Mill that commemorates Dickinsons' employees, thoughts turned back to unfinished business and the task of reconstruction. The restoration of electricity supplies to their pre-war standard in July, meaning no more power cuts, was a sign of life getting back to normal. Houses and streets had to be built and people urgently rehoused; there were squatters around the recently vacated US army camp in Cassiobury Park. Watford's only development of factory-built prefabs was put up in consequence in Gammons Lane to deal with the immediate acute housing shortage. Although they were meant as a temporary solution the two-bedroom bungalows were an improvement on some of the still existing poor pre-war housing stock, as they included a bathroom with flushing toilet (a luxury for those still using an outside toilet and tin bath) and a fitted kitchen. Only meant to last ten years, the prefabs lasted until the 1960s when the site was taken over by Holytree House for sheltered accommodation.

As well as repairing bomb damage to buildings and infrastructure the pre-war improvements to housing and road schemes had to be completed. The council appointed Clifford Sage as the new borough engineer with the formidable task of designing and building the required new housing estates, roads, public buildings, sewage systems and infrastructure. The county council were keen to restrict the town's growth but Sage who was an ambitious moderniser was in tune with the council and they had other ideas. They saw that it would be impossible to ignore the extra pressure on housing and services from returning servicemen with families and wartime workers who wanted to stay in the area. In 1946 the new Labour government passed a housing bill to begin a major building programme to replace old stock with modern high-quality council houses. The bomb damage to areas in London of poor housing was seen as an opportunity and to alleviate the housing shortage parliament passed the New Towns Act (1946) to facilitate new urban growth beyond the Green Belt; and Stevenage had the honour of becoming the first of the new towns. In the county Hemel Hempstead began its modern makeover as a New Town in 1947, followed by Welwyn Garden City and Hatfield in 1948. This did not remove the pressure on the Watford area to rehouse families from London and in 1947 land owned by the Blackwell family around Oxhey thought to be reserved for the National Trust was bought by the LCC and Oxhey 'New Town' was born.

By the 1950s municipal housing was being built at a fast rate and Watford too had its own developments such as the one at the intersection of the North Orbital Road and St Albans Road. The nearby estate of Kytes House, which had been used by the army in the war, was bought in 1949 by a Trust to build bungalows for the disabled in the grounds. Previously planned private developments were also completed including houses around Cassiobury Park and in the Bradshaw Estate and Bushey Lodge Estate off Bushey Mill Lane. Developments towards Garston and Leavesden for shops and housing meant to go hand in hand with the pre-war road improvements around Watford Bypass (A41) and the North Orbital (A405) road that had been put on hold were restarted. It was a sign of things to come as the area began to prosper from the 1950s onward, a growth that has continued to this day.

Schooling was not to go back to its pre-war normality. The Education Act passed in 1944 was implemented and schools like Leggatts Way School that had led the way would be the new standard. The old elementary schools were to be replaced by primary and secondary schools. The Act also introduced the tripartite system of state funded secondary education that included pre-existing grammar schools plus newly designated Elementary and Technical Schools. The building of the new College of Technology to replace the Watford Technical School in Queen's Road had been put on hold in 1939. Watford Technical College was eventually founded on its new site in Hempstead Road in 1947 but the building was not completed until 1953 when the college officially opened. Today the site is occupied by West Herts College. As evacuee children returned to their homes, the children of Reed's School who had been evacuated to Devon and Northampton did not return to their old Neo-Gothic asylum buildings. The governors decided to relocate the school to Basingstoke. The buildings, which had ceased to be used as a military hospital, were retained by the government as the headquarters for the Ministry of Labour. Today the Grade II listed buildings have been converted into flats and offices.

The government's planned National Health Service came into being in 1948. Health care within the region had to be rationalized and the demilitarized hospitals brought into the new system. Hill End reverted to its former role as a hospital for the treatment of mental and nervous disorders, although St Bartholomew's continued to control about one quarter of the beds for acute patients. The hospital closed in 1995. In Watford, the Watford and District Peace Memorial Hospital dropped 'and District' from its name and in 1965 it became an annex of Shrodells Hospital as part of Watford General Hospital. That same year Sir Geoffrey de Havilland, designer of the Mosquito, died there of a brain haemorrhage. The Peace Hospital closed in 1985 and the site is now occupied by the Watford Peace Hospice. Watford and District Isolation Hospital was renamed Holywell Hospital and became a specialist TB unit. It merged with Watford General in 1968 and was demolished twenty years later.

After the departure of its Canadian occupants, Leavesden Mental Hospital became part of the NHS under the control of the North West Metropolitan Regional Hospital Board as both a mental hospital and an institution for the mentally handicapped; there was an acute shortage of beds for both types of patients in the region at the time. For a time the Annexe building became the short-lived Leavesden Green Teachers' Training College and Asylum Road was renamed College Road. But in 1950 it was returned to Leavesden Hospital, renamed Abbots Langley Hospital and used to accommodate long-stay geriatric patients. In 1992 all its services were transferred back to Leavesden Hospital and the house was demolished, leaving only the lodge, and the grounds given over to redevelopment as part of Leavesden Country Park.

Immediately after the war everything looked set fair for the area's light industry. In a reprise of the previous war, returning soldiers were eager to return to their old jobs, and once again many women workers were required to stand aside. But unlike 1918, this was a time of economic growth bolstered by the government's social and restructuring programmes. This meant a growth in job opportunities for women in health and welfare as well as in administrative work. For many local industries peace meant a return to their previous activities. Cox & Co went back to manufacturing furniture with such success that it was said that every village hall in the country had a stack of their classic 'Cox-Chairs' and the company secured lucrative contracts to supply the new Heathrow Airport and Royal Festival Hall. The company sold up in 1980. London Transport's Aldenham Works turned from swords to ploughshares giving up Halifax bombers to become the more peaceful Aldenham Bus Overhaul Works where the worn out wartime bus fleet would be revamped. For other companies military contracts continued to be lucrative. WEMCO continued its switchgear production but became more dependent on naval contracts, hence its present configuration as Wippendell Marine. Scammell too continued to manufacture for the military but fell foul of rationalisation in the 1950s, becoming part of Leyland Motors. On the demise of British Leyland, the Dutch truck manufacturer DAF took over the company in the 1980s and the Watford plant was closed; the Tolpits Lane site has since been redeveloped for housing. Paper production thrived at the Dickinsons mills and the company grew to being one of the largest writing paper producers until they were bought out by asset-stripping investors in the 1990s. Although at first there were still paper shortages this did not hamper the print industry either. Odhams expanded its plant and activities and in 1954 work started on the massive new multi-storey 'No. 4 building', better known as the iconic Press Hall with its clock tower. Around the same time, Odhams pioneered the introduction of pre-printed colour into newspapers. But two large printing establishments in one town was to prove costly with a competition for labour. Sun Printers had also expanded, employing 3,600 workers in 1963. The growth could not be sustained. Odhams closed in 1969 leaving the Sun to carry on under various guises until the last printing presses rolled in 2004. In common with much of Britain, the manufacturing boom proved short-lived as the region began to lose its technological advantage combined with competition from cheaper wages abroad.

After its own initial burst of activity, the aircraft industry that had been so vital during the war, employing thousands of workers, also went through a turbulent time, suffering from increased foreign competition that led to numerous post-war reorganisations and reconfigurations. At Radlett aerodrome aircraft production continued with Hastings transport planes and Hermes airliners followed by the prototypes for the Victor bomber in the 1950s, and the Society of British Aircraft Constructors held airshows there in 1947 and 1948. When Handley Page went into liquidation in 1969, the airfield closed the next year. Leavesden was used for aircraft engine development and servicing, coming under the control of Rolls Royce until it closed in 1991. The airstrip was still used by civil flying organisations for general purposes flying until 1994; and then it was taken over by Warner Brothers and Leavesden Studios were born. De Havilland carried on innovating, resulting in the production of a number of important aircraft including the first commercial passenger jet airliner, the Comet. After a number of mergers, de Havilland became a member of the Hawker Siddeley Group, losing its separate identity in 1963. Today it is part of BAE Systems plc, the British aerospace and defence business. Whereas little remains of Radlett under its new guise as the site of an industrial estate, Elstree aerodrome continues as a flying club complete with its Second World War hangars.

The Americans returned Bovingdon aerodrome to RAF control in 1947, perhaps to the relief of some of the local villagers. The British Ministry of Civil Aviation took a share in the use of the airfield for civilian flying and during the '50s it was used as a military and civil maintenance facility. On 15 September 1949, the airfield was the starting point for a record-breaking air speed flight by a de Havilland Hornet to Gibraltar and back. In the 1960s, Bovingdon was used in the production of four Second World War films: *The War Lover* (1962), *633 Squadron* (1964), *The Battle of Britain* (1969) and *Mosquito Squadron* (1969). After the aerodrome closed in 1972 the facility still proved to be useful as a backdrop for a number of other film and TV sequences, including the Roger Moore outing as James Bond in *The Man with the Golden Gun* (1974) and the *Star Wars* spin-off *Rogue One* (2016).

The large requisitioned houses that had been the home to such mysterious goings on held on to their secrets for years. Few would remain in private hands and many would suffer a checkered post-war history. For Bucknalls, where the concept of a bouncing bomb was first trialled, little has changed as it continues as a building research centre under the title The Building Research Establishment. The Grove too carried on as a technical centre, though after the nationalisation of the railways in 1948 under various government transport bodies. Immediately after the war most of the LMS staff returned to their former headquarters in Euston, only a few remaining until the early 1960s. At first the building was used as a training college for the road haulage industry under the control of the British Transport Commission. At the end of the 1950s The Grove returned to railway control and the British Railways Board used the property for staff and management training, while in the 1960s giving over several of the wartime buildings to the Civil Engineering Training Centre. After the railways were privatized in the mid-1990s The Grove and its estate were sold off and turned into a hotel and golf course.

In 1949 Wall Hall became a teacher training college until its closure in 2003 for development into flats. Bushey Hall on the other hand continued its military connection, continuing to be used by the American Air Force during rising tensions with the USSR and the period of the Berlin airlift. In 1949 part of the land was sold off by its owners Spiers and Pond to continue as a hotel and golf course, while the rest was bought by the War Department and occupied by the RAF until 1953 when it was passed back to the USAAF who occupied it during the Cold War. The old hotel, affectionately known as 'the Castle', was demolished to ground level in 1955. Today the site and its old Nissen huts are home to the Lincolnsfield Centre and the '1940s Experience' where those too young to remember can feel a part of wartime Watford.

Acknowledgements

We would like to thank the staff and volunteers of the Watford Museum and the Bushey Museum, in particular Luke Clark and Ian Read, for their invaluable help. Bushey Museum kindly gave us access to their wonderful photographic archive. Watford Museum also host *Our Watford History*, a forum for sharing the history of the town. Hertfordshire County Council provide another forum, *Herts Memories*, and numerous local history groups have been a useful source of information: Abbots Langley Local History Society, Croxley Green History Project, Kings Langley Local History Society, North Watford History Association and the West Watford History Group. We would like to thank Alan Orchard of the Kingswood Residents Association for his cooperation in allowing the use of some of his reminiscences. Newspapers such as the now defunct *West Herts Post* and the *Watford Observer* past and present have proved useful.

Bibliography

'Abbots Langley Hospital' and 'Leavesden Hospital', *Lost Hospitals of London*, ezitis.myzen.co.uk/abbotslangley.html

Addison, Derek and Rock, Tony, *Bushey Hall and the Forties Experience*, Anchorprint, 2013

Atkin, Malcolm, *Fighting Nazi Occupation: British Resistance 1939-1945*, Pen & Sword, Barnsley, 2015

Bard, Robert, *Watford Past*, Historical Publications, London, 2005

Brayley, Martin, *The British Home Front 1939–45*, Bloomsbury, London, 2012

David Brooks, '"Third man" Kim Philby was nearly unmasked in St Albans', *The Herts Advertiser*, 19 May 2014

'Death of Jack Savage', *Flight International*, 27 September, Vol. 48, IPC Transport Press Ltd, 1945

Beney, Chris, 'Attenborough's Fields and Merryhill', Bushey and District Footpath Association, ramblers.org.uk/~/media/LBS/.../ Attenboroughs%20fields.pdf

Brown, Candy Kyler, 'What I Never Told You', *Remember History*, 2010, remember-history.com/my-heroes/oscar-mick-wagelie

'Charles de Gaulle's time in Hertfordshire', *Hertfordshire Life*, January 2017

Chown, Ron, 'My Early Days at the BBC', 2003, orbem.co.uk/misc/chown.htm

Chowns, Douglas, 'Boyhood Memories of Attenborough Fields in the 1940s', History Sheet No.38, Oxhey Village Environment Group, ouroxhey.org.uk

Cooper, John, *Watford through Time*, Amberley Publishing, Stroud, 2011

Daily Telegraph, 'Britain at War: War through the eyes of an Ascot family, 1939-46', excerpts from the diaries of Mrs Caroline Duckett, telegraph. co.uk

Dunlop, Lesley (ed.), *Ted Parish's Echoes of Old Watford, Bushey and Oxhey*, Past Days Publishing, Charmouth, 2013

'Elstree Aerodrome', *Royal Air Force Commands,* rafcommands.com/ archive/00606.php

'Foreign Tractors', *Engines of the Red Army in WW2*, o5m6.de/scammell. html

Forsyth, Mary, *Watford: a History*, The History Press, Stroud, 2015

Fry, Helen, *The London Cage: The Secret History of Britain's World War II Interrogation*, Yale University Press, London, 2017

Grace's Guide to British Industrial History, gracesguide.co.uk

Greenhill, Peter and Valentine, Pat, *The History of Sun Engravers and Sun Printers*, 2018, sunprintershistory.com

Hayward, James, *Double Agent Snow*, Simon and Schuster, London, 2013

Hemel at War, Hemel Hempstead School & Goldsmiths University of London, 2013, hemelatwar.org

Hertfordshire Archives and Local Studies, *Watford: Britain in Old Photographs*, The History Press, Stroud, 2012

Houlder, John M., CBE, 'History of Elstree Aerodrome', londonelstreeaerodrome.com

Jones, Robert, *Lewis Jones 1894-1953: a biography of the artist and fabric designer for the Silver Studio*, 2015

Jones, Robert, *Bob's Memoires*, 2015

Jonsson, Tommy and Olsson, Simon, *Agent Tate; the Wartime Story of Harry Williamson*, Amberley Publishing, Stroud, 2011

'Leavesden', *Airfields of Britain Conservation Trust*, www.abct.org.uk/airfields/airfield-finder/leavesden

London Orphan Asylum, childrenshomes.org.uk/LondonOrphan

Lovett, Dennis, (with Robert Heasman and David Wild), *The Grove Story*, British Railways Board (Double Arrow Club), 1984, rastall.com/grove

Marconi, Comitato Guglielmo, 'German Prisoners of War in Britain', 2012, radiomarconi.com/marconi/monumento/pow/pows.html

Masters, Christopher, 'Hertsmere Memories', hertsmemories.org.uk/content/herts-history/topics/wartime/bombed-in-the-war

Morgan, Rosemary, 'Wartime Experiences', Hands on History and Spring Park Films, 2016, springparkfilms.org.uk/Rosemary%20Morgan.pdf

Morriss, Agnieszka, *Broadcasts from the Błyskawica station during the Warsaw Uprising, 1944*, City University, London, 2017

Norton, Tommy, 'Playboy girls to rat bombs', *Borehamwood & Elstree Times*, 9 Dec 2005

Nunn, J.B., *Watford Past: a pictorial history*, J.B. Nunn, Watford, 1999

Orchard, Alan, 'Kingswood History', Kingswood Residents Association, krawatford.org.uk/history-page

'Outer London Defence Ring (Line A) Oct 2010', *Derelict Places: documenting decay*, derelictplaces.co.uk/main/ww2-defences/19307-outer-london-defence-ring-line-oct-2010-a.html

'Ovaltine', *Kings Langley Local History & Museum Society*, kingslangley. org.uk/ovaltine.html

Pawley, Edward, *BBC Engineering 1922-1972*, BBC Publications, 1972

Pells, Kelly, 'Watching the Blitz from Chorleywood Common', *Watford Observer*, watfordobserver.co.uk

Phillips, Oliver, *Watford in the 20th Century: Volume 2, South West Hertfordshire in the years 1939-1959*, The Watford Observer, Newsquest Ltd., London, 2012

Riding, Richard & Peerless, Grant, *Elstree Aerodrome: the Past in Pictures*, History Press, 2003

'Radlett', *Control Towers,* controltowers.co.uk/r/radlett.htm

Rickard, J, 'Leigh Light', 2007, historyofwar.org/articles/weapons_leigh_ light.html

Rook, Tony, *A History of Hertfordshire*, Phillimore & Co, Chichester, 1984

Rowdy, Terry, *Deceiving Hitler: Double-Cross and Deception in World War II*, Osprey Publishing, Oxford, 2013

Sanders, Ian, *UK Invasion Defences of WW2*, Pillbox UK, 2008, pillboxesuk. co.uk

Sainsbury, J.D., *Hertfordshire's Soldiers: a Survey of the Auxiliary Military Forces raised in Hertfordshire from 1757 to the Present Day,* Hertfordshire Local History Council, Hitchin, 1969

'Scammell', REME Museum of Technology, rememuseum.org.uk

Shields, Pamela, *Hertfordshire: Secrets and Spies*, Amberley, Stroud, 2009

Smith, Graham, *Hertfordshire and Bedfordshire Airfields in the Second World War*, Countryside Books, Newbury, 1999

Summerfield, Penny and Peniston-Bird, Corinna, 'Women in the firing line: the home guard and the defence of gender boundaries in Britain in the second world war.' *Women's History Review*, 9:2 (2000), pp. 231-55

The History of Sun Engraving and Sun Printers, sunprintershistory.com

'The Sandringham Road Bomb', North Watford History Association, north-watford-history.org.uk

Tonkin, Boyd, "Dad's Army: Discovering the deadly fighting force led by 'Britain's Che Guevara' Tom Wintringham", *The Independent Online,* 31 Jan 2016, independent.co.uk

Taylor, Richard Norton, 'How exploding rats went down a bomb – and helped British boffins win the second world war', *The Guardian*, 27 Oct 1999

Ward, Kate, 'Kenneth Martin Ward: episodes in a life (including memories of WWII)', compiled from Kenneth's notes and shared memories, March 2015, coleshillhouse.com

Waterson, Jill, *Odhams (Watford) Ltd (1935-1983)*, 2012, history-pieces. co.uk/Docs/Odhams.pdf

Watford Football Club Archive, watfordfcarchive.com

Watford Official Town Guide, Watford Borough Council, Ed, J. Burrow & Co, London, 1967

Wessex Archaeology, 'Land to the west of Radlett Aerodrome, Frogmore, St Albans: archaeological desk-based assessment', Environ UK, 2004

West, Nigel, *The A to Z of British Intelligence*, Scarecrow Press, Plymouth, 2009

Weiner, M-F and Silver, J R, 'Pierpont Morgan and the Wall Hall Estate during two World Wars', unpublished paper

White, Alice, *From the Science of Selection to Psychologising Civvy Street: The Tavistock Group, 1939-1948*, Doctor of Philosophy (PhD) thesis, University of Kent, 2016

Woolley, Randolph B., *Scarlet 42-5720 and Her Crew*, 2013, 306bg.us/ history/Plane_histories/Scarlet%2042-5720%20v2prt.pdf

Yaxley, Susan (ed), *The History of Hemel Hempstead*, Hemel Hempstead Local History Society, Hemel Hempstead, 1973

General Web Sites

Abbots Langley Local History Society, allhs.org.uk

Croxley Green History Project, croxleygreenhistory.co.uk

Herts Memories, hertsmemories.org.uk/content/herts-history/towns-and-villages/watford

Kings Langley Local History and Museum Society, kingslangley.org.uk/ history.html

Kingswood Residents Association, krawatford.org.uk/history-page

Our Watford History, ourwatfordhistory.org.uk/content/new-contributions/ ww2-in-watford

North Watford History Association, north-watford-history.org.uk

The National Archive, nationalarchives.gov.uk

West Watford History Group, westwatfordhistorygroup.org

Index